Revise

Edexcel GCSE
English Language and Literature
Foundation
Student Workbook

Janet Beauman
Alan Pearce
Racheal Smith
Pam Taylor

A PEARSON COMPANY

Contents

This Workbook is designed to help you focus your revision and provide support as you prepare for your Edexcel GCSE English Language and Literature Foundation Tier examinations.

Some students think that there is no need to revise for English examinations. This is simply not true! By making yourself familiar with the type of questions being asked and the mark schemes used by the examiner, you will increase your chances of performing to your full potential in the examination.

How to improve your revision technique

1 The first thing to do is to make use of your teacher, as they are a very valuable resource! Listen carefully to all the revision guidance and tips your teacher gives you in lesson time. If there is something you are unsure about, remember to ask. Your teacher may hold extra revision classes at lunchtime in the run-up to the examinations. If so, make sure you take advantage of this opportunity.

2 Check that you are familiar with what the examination papers look like, how many marks are awarded to each question and how much time you will have in each examination. There is guidance on this provided opposite.

3 The most effective way to revise is through active strategies. This means:
   • practising the skills you have acquired throughout the course
   • taking part in completing revision activities to consolidate your knowledge
   • comparing your answers with sample answers to see exactly where you can improve your performance. You can do this using this Workbook.

Using the Revise Edexcel GCSE English Language and Literature Foundation Student Workbook

This Workbook has been written to help you to revise the skills and knowledge that you will have covered in your GCSE English Language and Literature course. You may work through the book with your teacher within lessons. However, the activities in the Workbook are also suitable for you to complete during your own independent revision time.

 It has been designed for you to revise actively. There is room for you to write answers to activities and practise the skills required by completing sample examination questions. You are encouraged to highlight and annotate examination questions and texts as you might do in the examination itself.

The book is divided into three parts to reflect the Unit 2 Language, the Unit 1 Literature and Unit 2 Literature examinations. The tops of the pages are colour-coded to make it clear which part you are in.

As a reminder, here is a summary of the requirements for each Unit you will be taking:

English Language Unit 2: The Writer's Voice		
Time allowed		**Text allowed?**
1h 45 mins	**Section A: Reading**	Yes (clean copy)
	Section B: Writing	

English Literature Unit 1: Understanding Prose		
Time allowed		**Text allowed?**
1h 45 mins	**Section A: Literary Heritage**	Yes (clean copy)
	Section B: Different Cultures	

English Literature Unit 2: Understanding Poetry		
Time allowed		**Text allowed?**
1h 45 mins	**Section A: Unseen Poem**	
	Section B: Anthology Poems	Yes (clean copy)

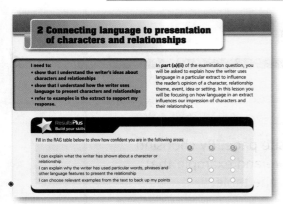

The following are some of the features that make this Workbook as user-friendly as possible:

- The lesson **introduction** will explain which part of the examination you will be revising for.

- **Learning objectives** at the start of each lesson explain what you will be aiming to achieve when answering this part of the examination.

- **ResultsPlus Build your skills** lists the skills you will be practising in the lesson and asks you to decide how confident you are with each of the skills listed – from red for 'not at all' to green for 'confident'. At the end of the lesson you will have the chance to review your confidence level again by filling in the same table. Your knowledge of the skills covered in the lesson should have improved.

- The **timer icon** gives a suggestion for how long you should spend on each activity. This is for guidance when working through the Workbook only - remember that this is not a suggestion for how long to spend on the examination question itself!

- **References** for extracts are included in this Workbook (e.g. chapter and page numbers) to allow you to look them up in your own copy and to re-inforce your knowledge of the text. These references are to the editions of the text which are listed as 'Prescribed texts' by Edexcel. Note that you will not be given a page reference for the extracts you are given in the examination question paper.

- **ResultsPlus Build better answers** give you an opportunity to read the mark schemes against which you will be assessed, and to match these to example student answers.

Finally, stay positive throughout your revision: think about what you can do, not what you can't. Good luck!

1 Identifying language features

I need to:
- **identify examples of a writer's use of language**
- **identify the language features used in these examples.**

In Section A of the examination you will answer three questions. Part (a)(i), part (a)(ii) and part (b). This lesson focuses on part (a)(i).

Part (a)(i) will ask you to give three examples of the writer's use of language in an extract and to identify the language feature used in each example.

ResultsPlus
Build your skills

Fill in the RAG table below to show how confident you are in the following areas:

	R	A	G
I can pick out examples of language features from an extract	○	○	○
I can comment on the effect of language features in an extract	○	○	○
I can explain how specific language features in an extract help to communicate a writer's ideas	○	○	○
I can choose relevant examples from the text to back up my points	○	○	○

Activity 1

15 MINS

1 Look at the definitions in the table on the opposite page. By choosing from the boxes below, select the language feature and example that goes with each definition. Write your answers in the table.

Language features

Noun	Personification
Verb	Simile
Adverb	Metaphor
Adjective	Colloquial language
Pronoun	Rhyme
Repetition	
Alliteration	

Examples

Quickly	As big as a bear
Run	The sun danced over the fields
She	The cold old farm
Green	The moggy is a goner
Rabbit	Snapped swiftly shut
	The darkest hour of the darkest night
	Her hair was silk

	Definition	Language feature	Example
1	The name of a person, place or thing		
2	A word that gives us more information about a noun		
3	A word that gives us more information about a verb		
4	A word showing action, movement or being		
5	Takes the place of a noun so that you don't have to repeat it		
6	Using two or more words close together that begin with or include the same consonant		
7	Language showing how people speak		
8	Comparing two things using a word such as 'like' or 'as'		
9	A comparison where something is said to be something else, without using a word such as 'like'		
10	Describing things that are not human as if they were		
11	Using the same word or phrase more than once		
12	Patterns of similar sounds		

Activity 2

15 MINS

1 Read **either** the extract from *Of Mice and Men* **or** the extract from *To Kill a Mockingbird* below. Find one or more examples of each of the language features listed in the table opposite and fill in the boxes with the examples you have found.

Of Mice and Men, Section 6, pages 114–115

Lennie removed his hat dutifully and laid it on the ground in front of him. The shadow in the valley was bluer, and the evening came fast. On the wind the sound of crashing in the brush came to them.

Lennie said, 'Tell how it's gonna be.'

George had been listening to the distant sounds. For a moment he was business-like. 'Look acrost the river, Lennie, an' I'll tell you so you can almost see it.'

Lennie turned his head and looked off across the pool and up the darkening slopes of the Gabilans. 'We gonna get a little place,' George began. He reached in his side pocket and brought out Carlson's Luger; he snapped off the safety, and the hand and gun lay on the ground behind Lennie's back. He looked at the back of Lennie's head, at the place where the spine and skull were joined.

To Kill a Mockingbird, Chapter 19, pages 199–200

'Well, I said I best be goin', I couldn't do nothin' for her, an' she says oh yes I could, an' I ask her what, and she says to just step on that chair yonder an' git that box down from on top of the chiffarobe.'

'Not the same chiffarobe you busted up?' asked Atticus.

The witness smiled. 'Naw, suh, another one. Most as tall as the room. So I done what she told me, an' I was just reachin' when the next thing I knows she – she'd grabbed me round the legs, grabbed me round th'legs, Mr Finch. She scared me so bad I hopped down an' turned the chair over – that was the only thing, only furniture, 'sturbed in that room, Mr Finch, when I left it. I swear 'fore God.'

'What happened after you turned the chair over?'

Tom Robinson had come to a dead stop. He glanced at Atticus, then at the jury, then at Mr Underwood sitting across the room.

In this extract Steinbeck uses the following language features	Examples from the extract
1 Adverbs	
2 Pronouns	
3 Colloquial language	
4 Adjectives	
5 Alliteration	

In this extract Lee uses the following language features	Examples from the extract
1 Colloquial language	
2 Repetition	
3 Pronouns	
4 Verbs	
5 Short sentences	

Activity 3

In part (a)(i) of your examination question, you will need to give three examples of the writer's use of language and identify the language feature for each of these examples.

1 Read **either** the extract from *Of Mice and Men* **or** the extract from *To Kill a Mockingbird* below and find three examples of the writer's use of language. Identify the language feature for each example you choose and record your answers in the table. An example from each text has been given to help you.

Of Mice and Men, Section 6, pages 114–115

Lennie removed his hat dutifully and laid it on the ground in front of him. The shadow in the valley was bluer, and the evening came fast. On the wind the sound of crashing in the brush came to them.

Lennie said, 'Tell how it's gonna be.'

George had been listening to the distant sounds. For a moment he was business-like. 'Look acrost the river, Lennie, an' I'll tell you so you can almost see it.'

Lennie turned his head and looked off across the pool and up the darkening slopes of the Gabilans. 'We gonna get a little place,' George began. He reached in his side pocket and brought out Carlson's Luger; he snapped off the safety, and the hand and gun lay on the ground behind Lennie's back. He looked at the back of Lennie's head, at the place where the spine and skull were joined.

A man's voice called from up the river, and another man answered.

'Go on,' said Lennie.

George raised the gun and his hand shook, and he dropped his hand to the ground again.

'Go on,' said Lennie. 'How's it gonna be. We gonna get a little place.'

'We'll have a cow,' said George. 'An' we'll have maybe a pig an' chickens … an' down the flat we'll have a … little piece alfalfa —'

'For the rabbits,' Lennie shouted.

'For the rabbits,' George repeated.

'And I get to tend the rabbits.'

'An' you get to tend the rabbits.'

Lennie giggled with happiness. 'An' live on the fatta the lan'.'

'Yes.'

Lennie turned his head.

'No, Lennie. Look down there acrost the river, like you can almost see the place.'

Lennie obeyed him. George looked down at the gun.

To Kill a Mockingbird, Chapter 19, pages 200–201

'Tom, you're sworn to tell the whole truth. Will you tell it?'

Tom ran his hand nervously over his mouth.

'What happened after that?'

'Answer the question,' said Judge Taylor. One-third of his cigar had vanished.

'Mr Finch, I got down offa that chair an' turned around an' she sorta jumped on me.'

'Jumped on you? Violently?'

'No suh, she – she hugged me. She hugged me round the waist.'

This time Judge Taylor's gavel came down with a bang, and as it did the overhead lights went on in the courtroom. Darkness had not come, but the afternoon sun had left the windows. Judge Taylor quickly restored order.

'Then what did she do?'

The witness swallowed hard. 'She reached up an' kissed me 'side of th' face. She says she never kissed a grown man before an' she might as well kiss a nigger. She says what her papa do to her don't count. She says, "Kiss me back, nigger". I say Miss Mayella lemme outa here an' tried to run but she got her back to the door an' I'da had to push her. I didn't wanta harm her, Mr Finch, an' I say lemme pass, but just when I say it Mr Ewell yonder hollered through th' window.'

'What did he say?'

Tom Robinson swallowed again, and his eyes widened. 'Somethin' not fittin' to say – not fittin' for these folks'n chillun to hear –'

'What did he say, Tom? You *must* tell the jury what he said.'

Example from extract	Language feature
dutifully	*Adverb*
afternoon *sun*	*Adjective*
1	
2	
3	

15 MINS

In your exam, part **(a) (i)** will ask you to read an extract you have been given and answer the following question:

> Give **three** examples of the writer's use of language in the extract.
> Identify the language feature for each example chosen.　　　(3 marks)

1　Read the two student responses to this question. The answers are based on the extracts on pages 10–11 of this workbook.

Of Mice and Men

Student A

Example	Language feature
bluer	Describing word
dutifully	Adverb
the evening came fast	

Student B

Example	Language feature
spine and skull	
	Adjective
	Repetition

To Kill a Mockingbird

Student A

Example	Language feature
'...offa...'	Language that sounds like speech
swallowed	Verb

Student B

Example	Language feature
'...hugged me. She hugged me...'	Repetition
	Short sentence

2　Decide how many marks (out of a total of 3) Student A and Student B would get. A mark can only be given if **both** an example is given **and** the language feature for the example is identified correctly.

3 Fill in the blanks below to explain the marks you have awarded.

Student A achieved a mark of _____ out of 3 because _____

_____

To improve their mark they could _____

_____

Student B achieved a mark of _____ out of 3 because _____

_____

To improve their mark they could _____

4 Select a different extract from the set text you are studying. Your teacher will be able to help you do this. Using this extract, spend 5 minutes finding three examples of language and then identifying the language feature for each.

Example 1: _____

Feature: _____

Example 2: _____

Feature: _____

Example 3: _____

Feature: _____

5 Now ask a partner to mark your answer or mark your own answer using the same criteria that you used in Question 2.

Results Plus
Build your skills

Fill in the RAG table below to see how your confidence has improved in the following areas:

	R	A	G
I can pick out examples of language features from an extract	○	○	○
I can comment on the effect of language features in an extract	○	○	○
I can explain how specific language features in an extract help to communicate a writer's ideas	○	○	○
I can choose relevant examples from the text to back up my points	○	○	○

2 Connecting language to presentation of characters and relationships

I need to:

- show that I understand the writer's ideas about characters and relationships
- show that I understand how the writer uses language to present characters and relationships
- refer to examples in the extract to support my response.

In **part (a)(ii)** and **part (b)** of the examination question, you will be asked to explain how the writer uses language in an extract to influence the reader's opinion of a character, relationship theme, event, idea or setting. In this lesson you will be focusing on how language in an extract influences our impression of characters and their relationships. It will be important that you have a full understanding of the text as a whole in order to understand the significance of the extract and to write a good answer.

ResultsPlus
Build your skills

Fill in the RAG table below to show how confident you are in the following areas:

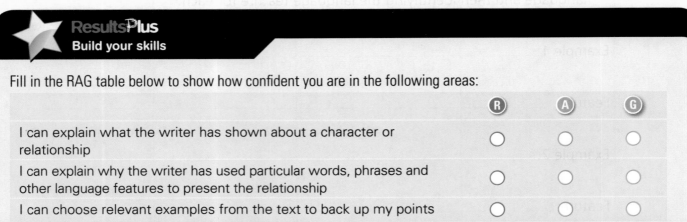

	R	A	G
I can explain what the writer has shown about a character or relationship	○	○	○
I can explain why the writer has used particular words, phrases and other language features to present the relationship	○	○	○
I can choose relevant examples from the text to back up my points	○	○	○

Activity 1

15 MINS

You will need to have a good understanding of the effects of different language features so that you can comment on the extract you are given in the examination.

1 Look at the table below which lists the effects of a range of language features. Now match the different language features given in red on the opposite page with the correct effects listed in green.

Language feature	Effect on reader
Verbs	will bring the text to life by showing action or movement
Short sentences	will deliver impact and make it seem as if an idea or thought is more important
Alliteration	will focus the reader on sound and create an atmosphere
Personification	will make the text dramatic and interesting or convey a certain mood. It helps the reader to relate to the object or idea that is being personified because it is easy for us to relate to something with human description
Questions	will get readers to think of an answer

Language feature	Effect on the reader
1 Commands	a will give the reader a further description of a person, place or thing
2 Repetition	b will show how people talk in the place where the text is set
3 Similes	c will show that the person using it has power and is getting someone to do something
4 Adjectives	d will help the reader see the comparison between one thing and another
5 Colloquial language	e will make it seem that an idea or thought is more important

2 Find four key words or phrases in your text that help to affect your view of either George (*Of Mice and Men*) or Atticus (*To Kill a Mockingbird*). Explain why you have chosen each word or phrase – how does it affect your view of the character? Write your answers in the grid below.

Word or phrase	How it affects your view of the character

Activity 2

15 MINS

1 Read the short extract below from the text that you have studied and answer the questions which follow. They will help you to think about how the language helps to present characters and/or their relationships. Remember that you won't get questions like this on an extract in the examination.

Of Mice and Men, Section 5, pages 94–95

She said, 'What you got there, sonny boy?'

Lennie glared at her. 'George says I ain't to have nothing to do with you – talk to you or nothing.'

She laughed. 'George giving you orders about everything?'

Lennie looked down at the hay. 'Says I can't tend no rabbits if I talk to you or anything.'

She said quietly, 'He's scared Curley'll get mad. Well, Curley got his arm in a sling – an' if Curley gets tough, you can break his other han'. You didn't put nothing over on me about gettin' it caught in no machine.'

But Lennie was not to be drawn. 'No, sir. I ain't gonna talk to you or nothing.'

She knelt in the hay beside him. 'Listen,' she said. 'All the guys got a horseshoe tenement goin' on. It's on'y about four o'clock. None of them guys is goin' to leave that tenement. Why can't I talk to you? I never get to talk to nobody. I get awful lonely.'

Lennie said, 'Well I ain't supposed to talk to you or nothing.'

'I get lonely,' she said. 'You can talk to people, but I can't talk to nobody but Curley. Else he gets mad. How'd you like not to talk to anybody?'

a What do we learn about Curley's wife when she says 'He's scared Curley'll get mad... gettin' it caught in no machine'?

_____

_____

b Find some examples of the use of questions by Curley's wife. What do these questions tell us about her character?

_____

_____

c What is the effect of the repetition 'I get awful lonely...I get lonely'?

_____

_____

**To Kill a Mockingbird,
Chapter 28, pages 267–268**

Jem knew as well as I that it was difficult to walk fast without stumping a toe, tripping on stones, and other inconveniences, and I was barefooted. Maybe it was the wind rustling the trees. But there wasn't any wind and there weren't any trees except the big oak.

Our company shuffled and dragged his feet, as if wearing heavy shoes. Whoever it was wore thick cotton pants; what I thought were trees rustling was the soft swish of cotton on cotton, wheek, wheek, with every step.

I felt the sand go cold under my feet and I knew we were near the big oak. Jem pressed my head. We stopped and listened.

Shuffle-foot had not stopped with us this time. His trousers swished softly and steadily. Then they stopped. He was running, running towards us with no child's steps.

'Run, Scout! Run! Run!' Jem screamed.

a What words or phrases in the extract show us that Scout is good at noticing things and thinks things through carefully?

_____

_____

b What words or phrases in the extract does Scout use to describe the person following them? How do these influence our view of her character?

_____

_____

c What do the references to Jem tell us about Scout's relationship with him?

_____

_____

Activity 3

20 MINS

In part (a)(ii) of the examination question, you need to explain how the writer's use of language in the extract influences the reader's impression of an aspect of the text. For example, the language might influence the reader's view of a character.

1   Look at the sample exam question below (either for *Of Mice and Men* or *To Kill a Mockingbird*) and re-read the relevant extract on page 10 or 11.

Of Mice and Men

Explain how the language in this extract influences your view of the relationship between Lennie and George.   (13 marks)

To Kill a Mockingbird

Explain how the language in this extract influences your view of Tom Robinson.   (13 marks)

2   Fill in the table below with four language features from the extract which would be relevant to support your answer to this examination question.

3   For each language feature, explain how it influences **either** your view of the relationship between Lennie and George **or** your view of Tom Robinson. One example for each text has been completed for you.

	Example from extract	Language feature	Effect on reader
	dutifully	*Adverb*	*This shows the reader that Lennie does what George asks and feels he should obey him.*
	'...she – she hugged me.'	*Repetition*	*The repetition of 'she' shows the reader that Tom is hesitating. He is scared to tell the court what really happened as he knows the reaction it will cause.*
1			
2			
3			
4			

In your response to part (a)(ii) of your examination question, you need to do four things to maximise your marks.

- Show that you **understand the text**. When you are explaining how language features influence the reader's impression of characters, their relationships, the setting or events, make sure your references to the text are accurate.

- Show that you **understand the writer's ideas**. This means you should explain the message the writer is trying to communicate and how he/she is trying to influence the reader's impression of the characters, events or setting, for example.

- Show that you **understand how the writer uses language features** to communicate his/her ideas. This involves identifying language features and explaining why they are effective.

- Give **relevant examples** of language from the text as evidence to support your points.

4   Now write one paragraph in response to the sample exam question on page 18, using the examples of language you have already identified.

Build better answers

1 Look at the relevant extract from a student response to the sample part (a)(ii) examination question on the previous page. Remember that the extract on which it is based is on page 10 or 11.

   a Underline the parts of the answer that show you the student understands the text, the writer's ideas or the writer's use of language.

   b Highlight any references to the extract that support the student's points. Don't highlight any irrelevant quotations!

   c Has the student made any mistakes? If so, circle them in red pen.

Of Mice and Men

George and Lennie are good friends. They use the word 'we' to refer to themselves which shows they are together. George and Lennie have had lots of problems to deal with. George is the oldest and because of this he tells Lennie what to do. Lennie wants George to take charge and make plans for them. He asks George to 'tell how it's gonna be'. Lennie repeats the things George says and this shows that he is listening to him. Verbs are used that show Lennie does as he is told like 'obeyed'. The language shows that Lennie is like a child.

To Kill a Mockingbird

Tom is not very educated and we see this in colloquial language like 'chillun' instead of children. He is nervous and because of this he swallows hard before he speaks. He repeats some of what he says. When he repeats 'she-she hugged me' it shows that he is hesitating because he is scared to tell the truth. He is nervous about being in court and being in trouble and the word 'nervously' shows how he is frightened in court. Tom is polite and doesn't want to repeat bad language because children might hear.

2 Look at the mark scheme below and decide which band the student response would fall into. Explain the reasons for your choice.

The student's answer is in Band _____ because _____

_____

_____

Band	Description
3	• Some understanding of the text • Some understanding of the writer's ideas • Some understanding of how the writer uses language • Occasional relevant reference to the extract to support response
4	• Generally sound understanding of the text • Generally sound understanding of the writer's ideas • Generally sound understanding of how the writer uses language • Mostly clear reference to the extract to support response
5	• Sound understanding of the text • Sound understanding of the writer's ideas • Sound understanding of how the writer uses language • Clear reference to the extract to support response

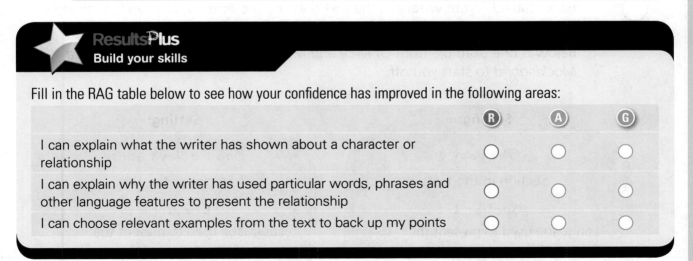

ResultsPlus
Build your skills

Fill in the RAG table below to see how your confidence has improved in the following areas:

	R	A	G
I can explain what the writer has shown about a character or relationship	○	○	○
I can explain why the writer has used particular words, phrases and other language features to present the relationship	○	○	○
I can choose relevant examples from the text to back up my points	○	○	○

3 Connecting language to presentation of setting

I need to:
- show that I understand the writer's ideas about a setting
- show that I understand how the writer uses language to present settings
- refer to examples in the extract to support my response.

In both **parts (a)(ii)** and **(b)** of Section A of the examination, you will be asked to comment on how the writer uses language in an extract to present a character, relationship, theme, event, idea or setting. In part (a)(ii) you will be given an extract, but for part (b) you will need to choose your own extract. In this lesson you will focus on how language in an extract influences our impression of a setting. It is important to understand the different settings within the text and how they are presented in order to comment effectively on the language in the extract.

ResultsPlus
Build your skills

Fill in the RAG table below to show how confident you are in the following areas:

	R	A	G
I can explain what the writer has shown about a setting	○	○	○
I can explain why the writer has used particular words, phrases and other language features to present the setting	○	○	○
I can choose relevant examples from the text to back up my points	○	○	○

Activity 1

10 MINS

1 Complete the spider diagram with the four most important settings in the text you have studied. Write **where** in the text they are presented and a brief summary of the language used to present each one.

Below is one example from *Of Mice and Men* and one example from *To Kill a Mockingbird* to start you off.

Setting:

The pool

Section in the text:

Section 1

Language used to present the setting: *Water described as 'warm' and 'tinkling'. Presents a very pleasant image of peace*

Setting:

Boo Radley's house

Section in the text:

Chapter 6

Language used to present the setting: *'Ramshackle' porch. Shows how the house is neglected.*

Setting:

_____

Section in the text:

_____

Language used to present the setting:

_____

_____

Setting:

_____

Section in the text:

_____

Language used to present the setting:

_____

_____

Language used to
present settings

Setting:

_____

Section in the text:

_____

Language used to present the setting:

_____

_____

Setting:

_____

Section in the text:

_____

Language used to present the setting:

_____

_____

Activity 2

1 Read the extract from the text you have studied and then answer the questions below to help you understand how the writer uses language to influence the reader's view of the setting. Remember that you will not have questions like this on the extract within your examination.

A few miles south of Soledad, the Salinas River drops in close to the hillside bank and runs deep and green. The water is warm too, for it has slipped twinkling over the yellow sands in the sunlight before reaching the narrow pool. On one side of the river the golden foothill slopes curve up to the strong and rocky Gabilan mountains, but on the valley side the water is lined with trees – willows fresh and green with every spring, carrying in their lower leaf junctures the debris of the winter's flooding; and sycamores with mottled, white, recumbent limbs and branches that arch over the pool. On the sandy bank under the trees the leaves lie deep and so crisp that a lizard makes a great skittering if he runs among them. Rabbits come out of the brush to sit on the sand in the evening, and the damp flats are covered with the night tracks of 'coons, and with the spread pads of dogs from the ranches, and with the split-wedge tracks of deer that come to drink in the dark.

a What is the effect of the adjectives such as 'warm', 'yellow' and 'golden' and the word 'twinkling'? How do they make the reader feel about this place?

_____

_____

b What is the language feature used in the phrase 'sycamores with mottled, white recumbent limbs…'? What is its effect?

_____

_____

c Look at the sentence beginning 'Rabbits come out of the brush…' What is the effect of the list of animals with repetition of 'and'?

_____

_____

d Choose one more example of a language feature in the text that influences the reader's view of the setting and helps convey the writer's ideas. Explain the reasons for your choice on a separate piece of paper.

To Kill a Mockingbird, Chapter 17, page 176

Maycomb Ewells lived behind the town garbage dump in what was once a Negro cabin. The cabin's plank walls were supplemented with sheets of corrugated iron, its roof shingled with tin cans hammered flat, so only its general shape suggested its original design: square, with four tiny rooms opening on to a shotgun hall, the cabin rested uneasily upon four irregular lumps of limestone. Its windows were merely open spaces in the walls, which in the summertime were covered with greasy strips of cheesecloth to keep out the varmints that feasted on Maycomb's refuse.

The varmints had a lean time of it, for the Ewells gave the dump a thorough gleaning every day, and the fruits of their industry (those that were not eaten) made the plot of ground around the cabin look like the playhouse of an insane child: what passed for a fence was bits of tree-limbs, broomsticks and tool shafts, all tipped with rusty hammer-heads, snaggle-toothed rake heads, shovels, axes and grubbing hoes, held on with pieces of barbed wire.

a The writer says the cabin rested 'uneasily' on four 'irregular' lumps of stone. What impression do these words give of the building?

_____

_____

b The writer says 'The varmints had a lean time of it, for the Ewells gave the dump a thorough gleaning every day.' 'Glean' means 'to pick over completely'. How does this influence the reader's view of the Ewells and their home?

_____

_____

c Find the simile in the second paragraph. What is the effect of the simile and the list of items that follows?

_____

_____

d Choose one more example of a language feature in the text that influences the reader's view of the Ewells' home. Explain the reasons for your choice on a separate piece of paper.

Activity 3

15 MINS

When you answer **part (b)** of the examination question, you won't be given an extract to look at. Instead, you will need to focus on an extract of your choice. This activity will help you to practise doing that.

1   Read the sample examination question for your text below.

Of Mice and Men

> In the novel, settings are important.
>
> Describe how the writer uses setting in **one other** part of the novel.
>
> You may wish to consider how the writer:
>
> • shows the details of the setting
>
> • shows the characters in the setting
>
> • describes the mood and atmosphere of the setting.   (24 marks)

To Kill a Mockingbird

> Maycomb has many different places where people live.
>
> Describe how a place where people live is presented in **one other** part of the novel.
>
> You may wish to consider how the writer:
>
> • describes the details of the place
>
> • shows the characters who live there
>
> • describes people's attitudes to the place.   (24 marks)

2   Choose a **short** extract from your text to help you answer the question. Remember, a setting can be outside or indoors. For example, it can be someone's private house, inside a public building, a street, a field or any part of a landscape. You might want to look back at your responses to Activity 1.

3   Read your chosen extract carefully. Pick out at least four examples of the writer's language and note down how these influence the reader's view of the setting.

When you answer the examination question, it is important to write about specific words and phrases from the extract in order to get a good mark. Ask yourself:

• Why did the writer choose this particular word, phrase or technique?

• How does it make me feel? What associations does it have?

• How does it affect my view of the setting?

Record your answers in the table opposite.

Extract:

	Example of language	How this influences the reader's view of the setting
1		
2		
3		
4		

4   Using the extract and examples of language you have already identified, write at least one paragraph of a response to the sample examination question on page 26. You might want to look back at page 19 to remind yourself of the things you should show in a response to both a part (a)(ii) and a part (b) question.

_____

_____

_____

_____

_____

_____

_____

_____

Build better answers

10 MINS

1 Remind yourself of the mark scheme which is shown opposite. Then look at the student answer to the question on page 26 that is shown below.

  a Underline text that shows the student understands how the writer has used language to present his/her ideas on setting.

  b Highlight any **relevant** examples used to back up the student's points.

Of Mice and Men

At the start of Section 5 the setting of the barn is described. He uses lots of good details to make the setting come alive. He describes the hay in the barn and tells us little details like the four-taloned Jackson fork. He makes it like we are there when he puts 'the heads of horses could be seen.' He tells us the day and time — it is Sunday and it is in the afternoon, 'the afternoon sun sliced through the cracks of the barn walls and lay in bright lines on the hay.' The word 'sliced' is good as it describes what it does on the floor. He also uses sounds of the horses with words 'nibbled, stomped and rattled,' two of these rattled and stomped are onomatopoeia which means words sound like what they are describing. This all helps us imagine what it looks like and you can imagine you are there in the barn with the horses.

To Kill a Mockingbird

An important setting in *To Kill a Mockingbird* is the Radley Place described in Chapter 1. Lee uses lots of good details to make the setting come alive like sharp curve and jutted. These words are quite sharp and show fear and danger. Lee describes the colour of the house and tells us little details like the green shutters. She makes it seem very dark be saying 'oak trees kept the sun away.' The Radley house is made to sound very frightening as she says a 'malevolent phantom' lives there. She also uses description to show that the house is neglected like the personification in 'the remains of a picket drunkenly guarded the front yard.' This all helps us imagine what it looks like and you can imagine you are there.

2 Look at the examples you have underlined and highlighted on the previous page. Which band do you think the student would get? Think about the following:

- Has the student explained how the writer presents the setting?
- Has the student explained the effect of specific language?
- Has the student included clear and relevant examples?

I would award the student a Band _____ because _____

_____

_____

Band	Description
3	• Some understanding of the text • Some understanding of the writer's ideas • Some understanding of how the writer uses language • Occasional relevant reference to the extract to support response
4	• Generally sound understanding of the text • Generally sound understanding of the writer's ideas • Generally sound understanding of how the writer uses language • Mostly clear reference to the extract to support response
5	• Sound understanding of the text • Sound understanding of the writer's ideas • Sound understanding of how the writer uses language • Clear reference to the extract to support response

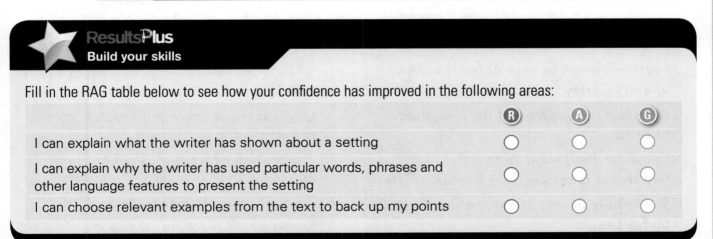

ResultsPlus
Build your skills

Fill in the RAG table below to see how your confidence has improved in the following areas:

	R	A	G
I can explain what the writer has shown about a setting	○	○	○
I can explain why the writer has used particular words, phrases and other language features to present the setting	○	○	○
I can choose relevant examples from the text to back up my points	○	○	○

4 Connecting language to presentation of ideas, themes and events

I need to:

- show that I understand the ideas, themes and events of the text
- show that I understand how the writer uses language to present key ideas, themes and events
- refer to examples in the extract to support my response.

Rather than commenting on a character, relationship or setting, you may be asked to comment on how the language in an extract influences our impression of an idea, theme or event. This lesson will help give you practice at doing this. Remember that in **part (a)(ii)**, you will be given an extract to comment on. In **part (b)** you will need to choose your own extract.

ResultsPlus
Build your skills

Fill in the RAG table below to show how confident you are in the following areas:

	R	A	G
I can explain what the writer has shown about a particular idea, theme or event	○	○	○
I can explain why the writer has used particular words, phrases and other language features to present key ideas, themes and events in the text	○	○	○
I can choose relevant examples from the text to back up my points	○	○	○

Activity 1

10 MINS

To get good marks in your exam, you need to have a good understanding of the whole text. You need to know what happens, and you also need to know about the novel's key ideas: what the writer wants the reader to understand, think and feel.

1 Complete the spider diagram with four of the key ideas, themes or events in the text and the language used to present them.

Idea, theme or event

Friendship

Section in the text:

Section 2 when George defends Lennie against Curley

Language used to present the idea, theme or event:

'Spose he don't want to talk?'
'We travel together,' said George coldly
Shows how George is determined to stand up for Lennie

Idea, theme or event

Race

Section in the text:

Chapter 12 where Calpurnia takes Scout and Jem to her church

Language used to present the idea, theme or event:

The warm bittersweet smell of clean Negro
'Why do you talk nigger-talk...?'
Shows how Calpurnia's world is different and strange to the children

Idea, theme or event:

_____

Section in the text:

_____

Language used to present the idea, theme

or event: _____

_____

Idea, theme or event:

_____

Section in the text:

_____

Language used to present the idea, theme

or event: _____

_____

Language used to present ideas, themes and events

Idea, theme or event:

_____

Section in the text:

_____

Language used to present the idea, theme

or event: _____

_____

Idea, theme or event:

_____

Section in the text:

_____

Language used to present the idea, theme

or event: _____

_____

Activity 2

15 MINS

1 Look at the extract from the text you have studied along with the part (a)(ii) sample examination question. Identify and then highlight four examples of language which will be relevant in answering the question.

**Of Mice and Men
Section 5, pages 92–93**

Explain how the language in the extract influences your view of Lennie's feelings.

(13 marks)

He unburied the puppy and inspected it, and he stroked it from ears to tail. He went on sorrowfully, 'But he'll know. George always know. He'll say, "You done it. Don't try to put nothing over on me." An' he'll say, "Now jus' for that you don't get to tend no rabbits!"'

Suddenly his anger arose. 'God damn you,' he cried. 'Why do you got to get killed? You ain't so little as mice.' He picked up the pup and hurled it from him. He turned his back on it. He sat bent over his knees and he whispered, 'Now I won't get to tend the rabbits. Now he won't let me.' He rocked himself back and forth in his sorrow.

**To Kill a Mockingbird
Chapter 10, pages 103–104**

Explain how the language in the extract influences your view of how the children's ideas about their father are changed. (13 marks)

Jem became vaguely articulate: ''d you see'd him, Scout? 'd you see him just standin' there?... 'n' all of a sudden he just relaxed all over, an' it looked like that gun was a part of him … an' he did it so quick, like … I hafta aim for ten minutes 'fore I can hit somethin'…'

Miss Maudie grinned wickedly. 'Well now, Miss Jean Louise,' she said, 'still think your father can't do anything? Still ashamed of him?'

'Nome,' I said meekly.

'Forgot to tell you the other day that besides playing the Jew's Harp, Atticus Finch was the deadest shot in Maycomb County in his time.'

'Dead shot…' echoed Jem.

'That's what I said, Jem Finch. Guess you'll change *your* tune now. The very idea, didn't you know his nickname was Ol' One-Shot when he was a boy? Why, down at the Landing when he was coming up, if he shot fifteen times and hit fourteen doves he'd complain about wasting ammunition.'

'He never said anything about that,' Jem muttered.

2 Now write two PEE (point, evidence and explanation) points to explain how two of these examples of language influence your view of Lennie's feelings (*Of Mice and Men*) or of how the children's ideas about their father are changed (*To Kill a Mockingbird*).

Remember that you need to:

- Make a point

- Give evidence to support your point, in the form of a quotation from the text

- Explain how the evidence affects your view

_____

_____

_____

_____

_____

_____

_____

_____

_____

_____

_____

_____

_____

_____

Activity 3

25 MINS

Below are two sample Section A part (b) examination questions.

1 Read the question for your chosen text and note down three possible sections of the text you could focus on in your response.

Of Mice and Men

In the extract, Lennie's feelings are presented.

Describe Lennie's feelings in one other part of the novel.

In your answer you should give examples of the language the writer uses. You may wish to consider how the writer:

- Gives details about Lennie's feelings
- Shows how other characters influence how Lennie feels
- Shows how Lennie's feelings affect other characters.

(24 marks)

To Kill a Mockingbird

In the novel, the children's changing ideas are important.

Describe how the children's ideas are changed in one other part of the novel.

In your answer you should give examples of the language the writer uses. You may wish to consider how the writer:

- Shows the situation the children are in
- Shows how they react to this
- Describes how the experience affects their ideas.

(24 marks)

Sections I could use to answer this question:

1. _____

2. _____

3. _____

2   Choose one of the extracts you identified opposite and find at least four language features that influence the reader's view of the idea or theme specified in the question.

Extract:		
	Example of language	**What this tells us about the idea, theme or event**
1		
2		
3		
4		

3   Now write at least two paragraphs of a response to the part (b) question opposite, using the language features you have already identified. You may want to remind yourself of the things you should do by looking back at page 19.

_____

_____

_____

_____

_____

_____

_____

_____

_____

_____

Build better answers

10 MINS

1 Remind yourself of the mark scheme (below) and read through your response to the sample examination question in Activity 3.

Band	Description
3	• Some understanding of the text • Some understanding of the writer's ideas • Some understanding of how the writer uses language • Occasional, relevant reference to the extract to support response.
4	• Generally sound understanding of the text • Generally sound understanding of the writer's ideas • Generally sound understanding of how the writer uses language • Mostly clear reference to the extract to support response.
5	• Sound understanding of the text • Sound understanding of the writer's ideas • Sound understanding of how the writer uses language • Clear reference to the extract to support response.

2 Think about how you might improve your response. Ask yourself the following questions, adding notes around your writing:

- Have you made points that are relevant to the question?
- Have you commented on why the writer has used specific language?
- Have you included enough relevant examples from the text?

3 Write down three things you could do to make your response better.

_____

_____

_____

_____

_____

_____

4 Rewrite parts of your response here, making improvements as necessary.

_____

_____

_____

_____

_____

_____

_____

_____

_____

_____

_____

_____

_____

_____

ResultsPlus
Build your skills

Fill in the RAG table below to see how your confidence has improved in the following areas:

	R	A	G
I can explain what the writer has shown about a particular idea, theme or event	○	○	○
I can explain why the writer has used particular words, phrases and other language features to present key ideas, themes and events in the text	○	○	○
I can choose relevant examples from the text to back up my points	○	○	○

5 Making the right decisions

I need to:

- **understand how to write for audience and purpose**
- **choose the most appropriate ideas for the audience and purpose.**

This lesson will help you to make the right choices in your writing task for Section B of the Language examination. In the examination you will be given a question that will include instructions for your writing. This lesson will help you revise what to do in response to the instructions in the question.

ResultsPlus
Build your skills

Fill in the RAG table below to show how confident you are in the following areas:

	R	A	G
I know what will interest different audiences	○	○	○
I know how to change my writing so that it serves the correct purpose	○	○	○
I can come up with appropriate ideas for tasks aimed at different audiences and purposes	○	○	○
I can put these ideas into a sensible order	○	○	○

Activity 1

You have to make choices depending on the **audience** for the piece of writing.

1. Complete the table below showing what you understand about the needs of the audience. You might want to use some of the words in the box to help you (they can each be used more than once):

> funny   formal   informal   chatty
>
> referring to shared experiences
>
> an impressive vocabulary   longer sentences   technical vocabulary

Audience	Language choice
friend	
teacher	
local politician	

2. Opposite is a paragraph written in very simple words and sentences. Rewrite this paragraph for each of the following audiences:

    a friend   **b** headteacher

    Make sure you make different choices each time.

When I get home from school I do my homework. It is important I get it done straight away. I find a lot of homework easy and I do not learn very much. Homework just takes up a lot of my time. I would like to be practising the guitar. I would also like to be riding at the local stables.

a friend

b headteacher

3 List the differences between the paragraphs you have written. Explain why you made these different choices.

You also have to make different choices depending on the **purpose** of the piece of writing.

Activity 2

10 MINS

1 Complete these sentences:

    a When I persuade I am trying to...

    _____

    b To review something I must...

    _____

    c When I am writing to argue I need to...

    _____

    d Commenting on something means I must...

    _____

    e When I am exploring an idea or issue I should...

    _____

2 The following phrases have been written with one of the above purposes in mind. Label them with the most appropriate purpose.

    a It is easy to see why homework is important. However there are many reasons why it might be considered a waste of time. _____

    b Homework is something that causes me great emotional turmoil. What is the point other than to upset me? _____

    c The current homework project is very successful. The choices that we were given helped to find something that was useful and interesting. _____

    d Homework is something that always causes difficulty, no matter which school you look at. _____

    e Overall, in my opinion, homework is something that has to be done. _____

Coming up with ideas is the most difficult part of the examination. You need to get really good at analysing the question to help you come up with ideas to write about. You need to think about the audience, purpose and subject of the piece of writing.

Look at this sample examination question, in which notes about the appropriate audience, purpose and subject are given.

Purpose: give a broad overview of the subject and cover different perspectives. Some personal opinion.

Audience: people who want to read about subjects that directly affect them on an everyday basis

Write an article for a lifestyle magazine in which you discuss the benefits and drawbacks of modern technology.

You may wish to include:

- details of how we use modern technology

- details about how modern technology has improved our lives

- what harmful effects modern technology might have

- any other ideas you may have   (24 marks)

Subject: how we use technology and give everyday examples of where it has a positive effect and where it has a negative effect

3   Now look at this sample examination question. Label the audience, purpose and subject and use these to come up with ideas in the same way.

Write an article for a teenage magazine in which you argue for or against the value of reality TV programmes. In your article, you may wish to include:

- Possible reasons for their popularity

- Possible benefits and possible negatives of reality TV programmes

- your own opinions of reality TV programmes.

- any other ideas you may have.

(24 marks)

Activity 3

20 MINS

You might find it useful to produce a spider diagram to help you come up with ideas. You should put the subject in the central circle and come up with as many ideas as possible, no matter how silly.

Look at this example:

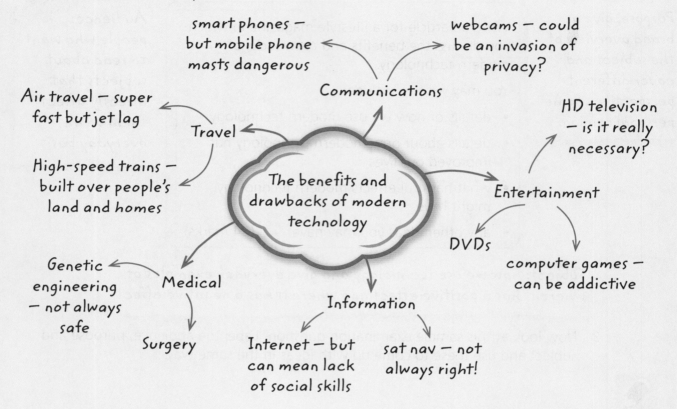

1   Look at the spider diagram above for the article on modern technology. Remember the purpose is to discuss and the audience is people who want to read about subjects that directly affect them. Sort through the ideas and complete this table:

	Good idea for the audience	Good idea because it will help text fulfil its purpose	Do not include

2 Now produce a spider diagram for the sample examination question from Question 3 in Activity 2 on page 41. Don't worry too much when you are producing your spider diagram. Write all your ideas down. Then, you should look through your ideas and select the ones that are most appropriate to the audience and purpose you have been given.

3 Now complete this table, selecting the ideas that are most appropriate for the audience and purpose of the question.

	Good idea for the audience	Good idea because it will help text fulfil its purpose	Do not include

Build better answers

Once you have come up with your ideas, you need to decide in which order to write about them.

15 MINS

1 You are going to use the ideas for the article on modern technology on page 42. You might want to use the ideas you came up with in Question 3 in Activity 3 on page 43 instead.

   a Put the ideas into an order that seems sensible.

_____

_____

_____

_____

   b Explain why the order you have come up with is sensible. You might want to start your explanation with:

> This idea is best to go first because...

_____

_____

_____

_____

The process that you have completed in this lesson is as follows:

- Look closely at the question
- Come up with ideas
- Identify appropriate ideas
- Put your ideas in order

This process will help you to:

- come up with effective ideas
- organise your ideas into paragraphs.

You will be marked on your ability to do both of these things.

2 Look at the plans opposite for the sample examination question from page 41. Each student has come up with different ideas and put them into a different order in their plan.

Decide which plan you think would get the best mark and explain your choice.

Plan 1	Plan 2	Plan 3
1 Reality TV is great 2 X-Factor 3 Why it is great 4 The next series and people's concerns	1 What is reality TV? 2 Why people like it 3 Why people think it is bad 4 Overall, my opinion – ok sometimes	1 Story about what they involve – give specific examples 2 The variety of attitudes to reality TV and why it is popular 3 Good and bad points – give specific examples 4 My opinion is...

I think Plan _____ would get the best mark because

_____

_____

_____

6 Choosing the right word

I need to:
- **choose words that are appropriate for the audience and the purpose**
- **choose words that will interest my audience**
- **check that these words are spelt correctly.**

This lesson will help you to choose words that will make your writing as interesting as possible. It is important to select words that are appropriate for your audience and purpose but it is crucial to engage your reader with clever choices.

ResultsPlus
Build your skills

Fill in the RAG table below to show how confident you are in the following areas:

	R	A	G
I can select words that are appropriate for audience and purpose	○	○	○
I can select words that are interesting for the reader	○	○	○
I am confident enough to select ambitious words even if I can't spell them	○	○	○
I can spell most words accurately	○	○	○

Activity 1

15 MINS

It is important to select words that are appropriate to the audience.

Here is a sample examination question.

> Write the text for a speech for parents in which you attempt to persuade them that there are many pressures on teenagers today.
>
> In your speech, you may wish to include:
>
> - examples of the pressures teenagers face
>
> - comparisons with the past
>
> - what can be done to help teenagers cope with pressure
>
> - any other ideas you may have.
>
> (24 marks)

1   Complete the paragraph opposite by circling the word from the yellow options that you think is most appropriate for the audience and purpose.

Your kids'/children's/teenagers' experience is incredibly/very different to what you lived through just a few years ago. Each day they are pushed/pressured/encouraged to work and behave in certain ways that you most likely have never imagined/believed/considered. School is all about results, friends are all about the right code of behaviour and family is about being cared for whilst looking mature/grown up/independent. There is no place where your kids/children/teenagers can relax, as they are always being judged/tested/pressured.

2 Here is another sample examination question.

> Write a letter to a friend in which you review a film they have said they would like to see.
>
> In your letter, you may wish to include:
> * basic details of the story
> * information about the camera-work or acting
> * whether or not you think they should go to see it
> * any other ideas you may have.   (24 marks)

Complete this paragraph by choosing words that you think are appropriate for the audience and purpose.

_____ John

I hear you would like to _____ the film Avatar! The film is

_____ . It is about some marines who are stealing resources

from a planet called Pandora. The story is _____ , John,

you are maybe going to find it a little _____ . However, the

_____ are _____ . You will love the way that you

seem to fly through the air with the aliens. It is _____ .

3 Explain the differences in the choice of words between the speech to parents and the email to a friend.

_____

_____

Activity 2

You need to select a variety of words to keep your text interesting for the reader.

1 Here is another paragraph from the review of the film *Avatar*. It is reviewing the actors in the film.

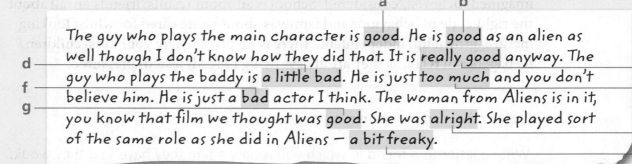

The guy who plays the main character is **good**. He is **good** as an alien as well though I don't know how they did that. It is **really good** anyway. The guy who plays the baddy is **a little bad**. He is just **too much** and you don't believe him. He is just a **bad** actor I think. The woman from Aliens is in it, you know that film we thought was **good**. She was **alright**. She played sort of the same role as she did in Aliens — **a bit freaky**.

Change the highlighted words or phrases. Use words or phrases that would offer more information to the reader. For instance, instead of 'a little bad' you might say 'poor', which is a more accurate use of words.

My alternative words:

a _____

b _____

c _____

d _____

e _____

f _____

g _____

h _____

i _____

2 When choosing words you need to be a little brave. You might know the perfect word but you might not know how to use it within a sentence.

Here are some words that you could have used in the paragraph about the actors that might entertain the reader more.

intense	sensitive	exaggerated
emotive	convincing	unconvincing
passable	talented	

Rewrite the paragraph using these words. You can use other words if you think you have better ones.

Activity 3

15 MINS

You will get some marks for spelling. Don't worry too much if you find it hard to spell more difficult words correctly; just make sure that you are careful to spell the easier words that you do know correctly.

1 Look through some of your exercise books from school. Make a list of all the words that your teacher has marked as being spelt incorrectly.

2 Look closely at this list of most commonly misspelt words:

address	guarantee	occurrence
advice	harass	piece
beginning	humorous	prejudice
believe	independent	privilege
changeable	jealous	receive
conscientious	knowledge	rhythm
conscious	leisure	separate
deceive	library	sincerely
definite	mediocre	special
desperate	miniature	surprise
disastrous	miscellaneous	thorough
embarrass	mischievous	through
fascinate	mysterious	truly
fiery	necessary	until
government	neighbour	weird
grateful	occasion	

a Highlight any interesting words that you think you would be able to use in a piece of writing.

b Tick any word that you know you can spell.

c Add any word that is not ticked to the list that you created in Question 1.

3 Choose a word from the list in Question 2 that you would not normally use. Try to write a sentence using the word. Check the meaning in the dictionary if you are not sure. Repeat the process for two other words on the list.

1

2

3

4 Produce a bookmark and write all the words that you need to pay special attention to onto one side of the bookmark. Use the bookmark in a book that you use all the time.

Build better answers

Here is the sample examination question again.

> Write a letter to a friend in which you review a film they have said they would like to see.
>
> In your letter, you may wish to include:
>
> - basic details of the story
> - information about the camera-work or acting
> - whether or not you think they should go to see it
> - any other ideas you may have.
>
> (24 marks)

1 Write the opening paragraph in response to this question, reviewing a film you have watched. You should focus on the words that you choose.

_____

_____

_____

_____

_____

_____

_____

_____

2 Read your paragraph. Use different coloured pens to highlight or underline:

  a words you are proud of

  b words that you think are not appropriate for the audience or purpose

  c words that you think could be replaced with something more interesting

  d words that you think are spelt incorrectly.

3 Make changes to your paragraph.

    a Change words so that they are more appropriate and more entertaining.

    b Change words that you think are spelt incorrectly. Listen to the sound of the word and make another attempt.

_____

_____

_____

_____

_____

_____

_____

_____

7 Choosing sentences

I need to:

- write sentences that are appropriate to audience and purpose
- write sentences that are interesting for the reader
- remember to use correct punctuation.

This lesson will help you to write in sentences. It is obviously important to use punctuation in your sentences but you need to be able to use punctuation so that it has an impact on your audience. This lesson will also help you to write appropriate and interesting sentences.

ResultsPlus
Build your skills

Fill in the RAG table below to show how confident you are in the following areas:

	R	A	G
I can write sentences that are fit for audience and purpose	○	○	○
I can vary the length of sentences that I write in order to interest the reader	○	○	○
I can vary the kinds of sentence I write in order to interest the reader	○	○	○
I can use punctuation to divide my work into sentences	○	○	○
I can use punctuation to add meaning to my work	○	○	○

Activity 1

20 MINS

At the most basic level you should be careful to put full stops and capital letters in your work. You should practise checking your work.

1   Here is a paragraph where no sentences have been marked. Insert full stops and capital letters.

school uniform is meant to make life easier for students they are less

likely to get bullied and they don't have to buy expensive clothes however

there is the cost of uniform and the fact that people deserve to have some

choice in what they wear some schools try to balance uniform and students' own clothes by wearing a casual top but all this does is make

people look untidy it seems that there is no easy answer when it comes

to school uniform

2 You also need to be able to use other types of punctuation. The mark scheme asks you to use a variety of punctuation. You need to try to use question marks, exclamation marks and commas.

Complete these sentences with the appropriate punctuation:

a Why do headteachers insist on school uniform

b It is not true

c Wearing uniform does not prevent bullying as any student will tell you people are still capable of making you feel different even when you look the same

3 Rewrite the paragraph about school uniform from Question 1. Include the different sentences you have just completed.

_____

_____

_____

_____

_____

_____

4 Read the paragraph with only full stops in Question 1. Now read the paragraph with the new sentences that include a question mark, exclamation mark and some commas in Question 3. How do they change the 'feel' of the writing?

_____

_____

_____

Activity 2

10 MINS

In the examination, you need to write in a way that is suitable for the audience and purpose. To make your writing interesting, you should try to vary the kinds of sentence you use. Here are some tips:

Exclamations

These are sentences that end in an exclamation mark.

- Exclamations can be used to emphasise a point – but don't use them too often.
- Exclamations can be used to show that you think something is surprising or amazing.
- *Don't* use these in very formal pieces of writing.
- *Do* use these in informal writing.

Questions

These are sentences that end in a question mark. If the person reading is not actually going to answer the question (e.g. if it is in a newspaper article) it is called a **rhetorical question**.

- Use rhetorical questions to get the reader to think about an issue.
- Rhetorical questions engage the reader's interest and can make your writing more interesting.
- Rhetorical questions are very useful when you are writing to persuade or to argue.

Sentence length

It is a good idea to vary the length of your sentences. This will make your writing flow better.

- Use a short sentence after a long sentence to emphasise a point.
- If you use long sentences, check you have included correct punctuation.

1 Read the tips above. Now look at the extract below. It has been written to argue that school uniform is a good thing.

> Most teenagers are interested in fashion and like to express themselves through their clothes. But most schools still have school uniform. There are several reasons for this. If everybody has to wear the same clothes then nobody will pick on students who are less fashionable, or can't afford the latest clothes.

a Replace one of the sentences with a rhetorical question.

_____

b Read the paragraph again and explain the effect of the rhetorical question on the writing as a whole.

_____

_____

2 Read the paragraph below. It is the opening paragraph of an article in a teenage magazine reviewing the fitness activities available to young people in the town of Holmethorpe. The audience is young people in the local area.

> Sometimes it seems like there's not much to do, but actually Holmethorpe is packed full of surprising activities if you look for them. Whenever you next feel bored, check out the local sports club which runs all kinds of classes from football to dance and from cross-country to boules. Even javelin-throwing is on the agenda. If you're feeling very adventurous take a visit to the climbing wall where you can get a reduced young-person rate for an hour of clambering with a personal instructor. Guaranteed to get you active.

a Add in an exclamation mark.

b Change the punctuation to vary the length of the sentences. You can change words if you need to do so.

c Read the new paragraph and explain the effect of the changes you have made.

_____

_____

Activity 3

20 MINS

To use sentences well you need to:

- use a variety of sentences – long and short, questions and exclamations
- use accurate punctuation.

Here is a sample examination question.

> Write an article for the school website reviewing the facilities available to young people in your local area.
>
> In your article, you may wish to include:
>
> - details about the facilities
> - quotes from people who use the facilities, giving their opinions
> - your own opinion about the facilities and ideas on improvements that could be made
> - any other ideas you may have.
>
> (24 marks)

1 Write a paragraph in response to this examination question. Remember to think about the audience (students) and purpose (to review).

_____

_____

_____

_____

_____

_____

_____

_____

_____

_____

2 Read your paragraph again.

- Have you included sentences of different lengths?

- Could you include a rhetorical question?

- Could you include an exclamation? Is it appropriate?

- Is the writing appropriate for your audience (students)? Is it appropriate for the purpose (to review)?

Make changes to your paragraph below.

_____

_____

_____

_____

_____

_____

_____

3 Re-read your paragraph. Is the punctuation accurate? Make any necessary corrections.

_____

_____

_____

_____

_____

_____

_____

Build better answers

In the examination, you get some marks for being interesting and some marks for being accurate.

1 Read the following paragraphs. They are extracts from student answers to the sample examination question on page 62.

Student A

The first performance of the school musical 'The Wiz' was on Friday.

Over 70 people came to see the performence. The performence was in the school hall. Everybody thought it was really good. The audience really enjoyed the singing and dancing. Chantelle Pryce was brilliant as Dorothy.

Andrea Furlong was also great as Aunt Em she had to play an old lady, which must have been difficult.

Student B

On Friday, over 70 people came to see the first performance of 'The Wiz' in the school hall. Everybody thought it was excelent, and the audience seemed to particularly enjoy the singing and dancing. Chantelle Pryce was brilliant as Dorothy and Andrea Furlong was also great as Aunt Em. She had an especially tough role as she had to play an old lady!

a Can you spot any mistakes in the paragraphs? Highlight each one.

b Which paragraph do you think is more interesting? Explain your reasons.

Student _____ 's paragraph is more interesting because

_____

_____

_____

2 Explain in your own words what you need to remember to do when writing and editing sentences.

_____

_____

_____

_____

Fill in the RAG table below to show how your confidence has improved in the following areas:

	R	A	G
I can write sentences that are fit for audience and purpose	○	○	○
I can vary the length of sentences that I write in order to interest the reader	○	○	○
I can vary the kinds of sentence I write in order to interest the reader	○	○	○
I can use punctuation to divide my work into sentences	○	○	○
I can use punctuation to add meaning to my work	○	○	○

8 Making best use of paragraphs

I need to:
- **write in paragraphs**
- **link paragraphs together**
- **develop ideas within paragraphs.**

This lesson will help you to organise your ideas within your writing. Once you have decided which ideas to include in your writing, you need to think of a basic paragraph structure. For each new idea you should use a new paragraph. Your job when you are writing is to make the ideas in these paragraphs clear and to make sure they all combine together to make one whole piece of writing.

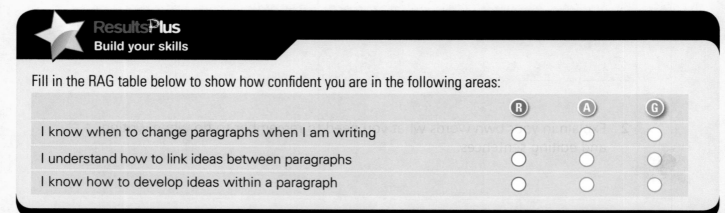

Results Plus
Build your skills

Fill in the RAG table below to show how confident you are in the following areas:

	R	A	G
I know when to change paragraphs when I am writing	○	○	○
I understand how to link ideas between paragraphs	○	○	○
I know how to develop ideas within a paragraph	○	○	○

Activity 1

10 MINS

This activity will refresh your memory about what to do when you first enter the examination. Here is a sample examination question.

> Write a review for the school magazine focused on a recent school event such as a sports team's performance or a recent production.
>
> In your review, you may wish to include:
>
> - a description of the event
>
> - anything significant that happened at the event
>
> - your own opinion about the event
>
> - any other ideas you may have.　　　　(24 marks)

1   Label the question on page 62, making notes on the audience, purpose and subject of the piece of writing.

2   Now draw a spider diagram. Come up with as many ideas as you can.

3   List the four ideas you are going to use and the order in which you are going to write about them.

_____

_____

_____

_____

You now have the four topics for the four paragraphs you are going to write in your response to the examination question. This is called a paragraph map.

10 MINS

Here is a sample examination question.

> Write the text for a speech for parents in which you persuade them that they should support a charity you feel strongly about.
>
> In your speech you may wish to include:
>
> - information about what the charity does
> - why you think it is important
> - how parents can help
> - any other ideas you think are important.   (24 marks)

Here is a sample paragraph map for this question:

> **Paragraph 1** Welcome the parents and explain why they have always been helpful in the past
>
> **Paragraph 2** Give background to charity
>
> **Paragraph 3** Explain why help is needed so much now
>
> **Paragraph 4** Ask for their help and give examples how

The best way to make sure the reader understands what the paragraph is going to be about is to use a topic sentence at the start of the paragraph. For instance:

> *I would like to welcome our generous parents to this charity event this evening.*

1   Write a topic sentence for each of the remaining three paragraphs.

Topic sentence 2:

_____

_____

Topic sentence 3:

_____

_____

Topic sentence 4:

_____

_____

You then need to be able to develop the main idea of the paragraph by giving reasons, descriptions and examples. For instance:

An example **Some description**

> I would like to welcome our generous parents to this charity event this evening. In the past you have always supported us fully in our aims and for this we are grateful. There was the huge effort when we chose to walk the length of the UK, thanks especially to the Jacksons for following me so closely with the van that served drinks! There was also the massive fair we held on the field that produced funds for the new sports centre. I know some of you parents have got much fitter thanks to this: so maybe not so selfless!

Another example **A reason**

2 Write the second paragraph for this piece of writing. Develop the idea in the paragraph by giving reasons, descriptions and examples.

_____

_____

_____

_____

_____

_____

_____

_____

_____

_____

Activity 3

20 MINS

You need to link your paragraphs together so that they flow to become one piece of writing. The easiest way to do this is to use connectives such as:

- firstly
- in conclusion
- also
- on the other hand
- however
- yet
- it could also be said

1 Rewrite your topic sentences from Activity 2 to include connectives. For instance:

However, more help is needed from you today!

Topic sentence 2:

_____

_____

Topic sentence 3:

_____

_____

Topic sentence 4:

_____

Another technique you can use is a question. For instance, at the end of the first paragraph you could write:

So, you're thinking: what do they want us to do now?

2 Use a question at the end of the second paragraph you wrote in Activity 2. Use the question to introduce the idea that is coming in the next paragraph.

_____

_____

Finally, you can use key words at the beginning of the next paragraph that repeat ideas that have been used in the previous paragraph. For instance, the second paragraph could begin:

> I am hoping the Jackson family are ready to follow me again as we take on an even bigger challenge than walking through the countryside!

This helps to link and structure your writing effectively.

3 Write the third paragraph for this examination response below. Use key words from the second paragraph to help introduce ideas in this paragraph.

_____

_____

_____

_____

_____

_____

_____

_____

_____

_____

_____

_____

_____

Build better answers

Here is a sample examination question:

> Write a letter to your local newspaper suggesting how your neighbourhood could be improved.
>
> In your letter you may wish to include:
>
> - reasons why your local area needs to be improved
> - your suggestions for improvements
> - how local people and the local area would benefit
> - any other ideas you may have.   (24 marks)

1 a Label the question with notes on the content you will include that is appropriate for audience, purpose and subject.

   b Create a spider diagram on a separate sheet of paper with further ideas.

   c Draw up a paragraph map below.

Paragraph 1 _____

Paragraph 2 _____

Paragraph 3 _____

Paragraph 4 _____

2 Write the opening two paragraphs for your response to this question.

_____

_____

_____

_____

_____

_____

_____

_____

_____

_____

3 Re-read your paragraphs and answer these questions:

    a Have I remembered to start each paragraph on a new line? ☐

    b Have I used topic sentences to introduce the key idea in the paragraph? ☐

    c Have I used examples, reasons and descriptions to develop ideas? ☐

    d Have I used connectives or key words to link the paragraphs? ☐

    e Have I used a question to help to introduce the idea in the next paragraph? ☐

1 Summarising events

I need to:

- show that I know what the key events are
- select appropriate events and place them in the right order.

This lesson will help you to prepare for the Section A Literary Heritage question in your Unit 1 Literature examination. There are four parts to the question:

- **Part (a)** will ask you to outline key events leading up to or following an extract
- **Part (b)** will ask you to comment on the writer's use of language in the extract
- **Part (c)** will ask you to comment on what you learn about one of the characters from the extract
- **Part (d)** will ask you to comment on another section of the text that you will need to choose.

This lesson focuses on part (a) of the examination question – outlining key events that occur before or after an extract you will be given.

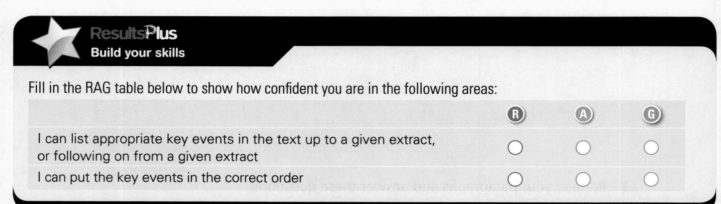

ResultsPlus
Build your skills

Fill in the RAG table below to show how confident you are in the following areas:

	R	A	G
I can list appropriate key events in the text up to a given extract, or following on from a given extract	○	○	○
I can put the key events in the correct order	○	○	○

Activity 1

10 MINS

1 Look at the list of events in the text you have been studying. Number them in the correct order.

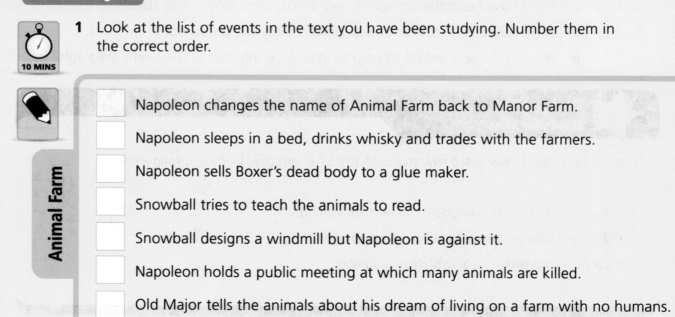

Animal Farm

	Napoleon changes the name of Animal Farm back to Manor Farm.
	Napoleon sleeps in a bed, drinks whisky and trades with the farmers.
	Napoleon sells Boxer's dead body to a glue maker.
	Snowball tries to teach the animals to read.
	Snowball designs a windmill but Napoleon is against it.
	Napoleon holds a public meeting at which many animals are killed.
	Old Major tells the animals about his dream of living on a farm with no humans.

Dr Jekyll and Mr Hyde

☐ Poole tells Utterson that Jekyll has locked himself into his laboratory for more than a week.

☐ Jekyll loses his ability to change back from Hyde.

☐ A girl sees Hyde kill an old man in the street.

☐ Enfield tells Utterson about how Hyde trampled over a young girl in the street.

☐ Lanyon dies because he has seen Hyde turn into Jekyll.

☐ Guest thinks that Jekyll and Hyde's handwriting are similar.

☐ Utterson watches a building that he knows Hyde often goes to.

2 Add three more key events to the list. You can write your full list in the correct order below.

_____

_____

_____

_____

_____

_____

_____

_____

_____

_____

Activity 2

25 MINS

In the examination, part (a) will ask you to outline **either** the key events leading up to **or** the key events following on from a printed extract from the text you will be given. Examples of both types of question are given here and on page 74. You may also be given a key event from your text that will be the starting point or finishing point for the key events you are asked to outline.

1 Read the extract below from the text you have studied and outline the key events that are asked for.

Animal Farm, Chapter 5, page 35

> Outline the key events **from** when the milk disappeared **up to** this extract.
>
> (10 marks)

Afterwards Squealer was sent around the farm to explain the new arrangements to the others.

'Comrades,' he said, 'I trust that every animal here appreciates the sacrifice that Comrade Napoleon has made in taking this extra labour upon himself. Do not imagine, comrade, that leadership is a pleasure! On the contrary, it is a deep and heavy responsibility. No one believes more firmly than Comrade Napoleon that all animals are equal. He would be only too happy to let you make your decisions for yourselves. But sometimes you might make the wrong decisions, comrades, and then where should we be? Suppose you had decided to follow Snowball, with his moonshine of windmills – Snowball, who, as we now know, was no better than a criminal?'

Dr Jekyll and Mr Hyde, 'Search for Mr Hyde', page 14

> Outline the key events that **lead up** to this extract.   (10 marks)

And at last his patience was rewarded. It was a fine dry night; frost in the air; the streets as clean as a ballroom floor; the lamps, unshaken by any wind, drawing a regular pattern of light and shadow. By ten o'clock, when the shops were closed, the bystreet was very solitary and, in spite of the low growl of London from all round, very silent. Small sounds carried far; domestic sounds out of the houses were clearly audible on either side of the roadway; and the rumour of the approach of any passenger preceded him by a long time. Mr Utterson had been some minutes at his post, when he was aware of an odd, light footstep drawing near.

When you outline the **key** events in the text, it is important to make sure that events really are relevant and significant.

2 Look back at your answer. Have you included only key events? Make any changes to your list above that you feel are necessary.

Activity 3

15 MINS

In the examination you may be asked to outline events **from** the extract that you are given **until** a later point in the text.

1 Read the extract which follows from the text you have studied and outline the key events that are asked for.

Animal Farm, Chapter 5, pages 33–34

Outline the key events that **follow on** from this extract **up to** the end of Chapter 8 when the Fifth Commandment, about drinking alcohol, has been altered. (10 marks)

By the time he had finished speaking, there was no doubt as to which way the vote would go. But just at this moment Napoleon stood up and, casting a peculiar side-long look at Snowball, uttered a high-pitched whimper of a kind no one had ever heard him utter before.

At this there was a terrible baying sound outside, and nine enormous dogs wearing brass-studded collars came bounding into the barn. They dashed straight for Snowball, who only sprang from his place just in time to escape their snapping jaws. In a moment he was out of the door and they were after him.

Dr Jekyll and Mr Hyde, 'Doctor Jekyll was Quite at Ease', pages 19–20

Outline the key events that **follow on** from this extract **up to** Lanyon's death in the chapter 'Remarkable Incident of Doctor Lanyon'. (10 marks)

The large handsome face of Dr Jekyll grew pale to the very lips, and there came a blackness about his eyes. 'I do not care to hear more,' said he. 'This is a matter I thought we had agreed to drop.'

'What I heard was abominable,' said Utterson.

'It can make no change. You do not understand my position,' returned the doctor, with a certain incoherency of manner. 'I am painfully situated, Utterson; my position is a very strange – a very strange one. It is one of those affairs that cannot be mended by talking.'

'Jekyll,' said Utterson, 'you know me: I am a man to be trusted. Make a clean breast of this in confidence; and I make no doubt I can get you out of it.'

2 Now look back at your answer. Ensure you have listed only key events and also included all those which occur only within the section specified. Make any changes to your list above that you feel are necessary.

Build better answers

1 Look at the extract from the text you have studied on page 74. Then read the sample examination question given and the student response that appears after it.

Animal Farm

> Outline the key events **from** the end of the battle of the cowshed **up until** this extract. **(10 marks)**
>
> - At the end of the battle, Boxer thought that he had killed a stable-lad.
> - Snowball says that the only good human is a dead human.
> - Snowball and Boxer are awarded a medal 'Animal Hero, First Class'.
> - Mr Jones' gun is found and the animals set it up at the bottom of the flagpole.
> - Mollie ran away from Animal farm.
> - Debates took place on the farm, with Snowball and Napoleon disagreeing on everything.
> - Napoleon taught the sheep to bleat 'Four legs good, two legs bad.'
> - Snowball designed a windmill.
> - Napoleon urinated over the plans.

Dr Jekyll and Mr Hyde

> Outline the key events **from** the beginning of the chapter 'Search for Mr Hyde' **up until** this extract. **(10 marks)**
>
> - Although it was after midnight Utterson went to see his friend Dr Lanyon to talk about Jekyll.
> - Utterson and Lanyon talk about Jekyll. Lanyon says he fell out with Jekyll because of Jekyll's scientific ideas.
> - Utterson went home and worried about the story that Lanyon had told him about Hyde knocking over a young girl and then ignoring her.
> - Utterson spent many nights waiting outside in order to meet Hyde.
> - Utterson meets Hyde. He asks to see Hyde's face.
> - Utterson tells Hyde that he is a friend of Jekyll. Hyde is shocked.
> - Utterson goes round to Jekyll's house but Jekyll is out so Utterson talks to his servant Poole about Hyde.
> - Utterson is worried that Hyde will kill Jekyll.
> - Jekyll invited some friends around for a meal.
> - After everyone else has gone Utterson tells Jekyll of his concerns about Hyde and the will.

2 Using the mark scheme, decide which band the student response would fall into and explain your reasons.

Band	Description
3	• Selection of appropriate key events is occasionally sound • Chronology of key events is occasionally accurate
4	• Selection of appropriate key events is generally sound • Chronology of key events is mostly accurate
5	• Selection of appropriate key events is sound • Chronology of key events is fully accurate

I think the student's response would fall into Band _____ because _____

_____

_____

ResultsPlus
Build your skills

Fill in the RAG table below to see how your confidence has improved in the following areas:

	R	A	G
I can list appropriate key events in the text up to a given extract, or following on from a given extract	○	○	○
I can put the key events in the correct order	○	○	○

2 Responding to characters

I need to:

- **show that I have a sound understanding of the characters**
- **select appropriate examples from the text to demonstrate my knowledge of the characters.**

This lesson will help you to prepare for the **part (c)** of the Section A Literary Heritage question in your examination. You will be given an extract from the text you have studied – the same extract as you used for part (a) – and you will be asked to comment on what you learn about one of the characters from the extract. You need to have a good knowledge of the characters in the text you have studied in order to write a good response on the extract for part (c).

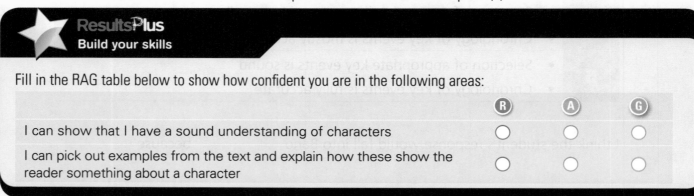

ResultsPlus
Build your skills

Fill in the RAG table below to show how confident you are in the following areas:

	R	A	G
I can show that I have a sound understanding of characters	○	○	○
I can pick out examples from the text and explain how these show the reader something about a character	○	○	○

Activity 1

5 MINS

1 To check your knowledge, complete the paragraph about the text you have studied, using the words from the box below.

Animal Farm

Squealer is a _____ talker. He works with Snowball and Napoleon to create Animalism. Because many of the animals are not clever enough to learn the Commandments, Squealer teaches them _____ His job on Animal Farm is to explain that nothing that Napoleon does is selfish. For example, he explains that the pigs ate the _____ to keep healthy so that they could run the farm effectively. The alternative, he explains, would be to have _____ back. When Napoleon announces that there will be no more _____ Squealer is sent round the farm to explain the new arrangements. He argues that leadership is a huge _____ and the animals can't be allowed to make decisions themselves because they might make the _____ decisions. Squealer's _____ helps to persuade the animals that everything on the farm is fine and that Napoleon is continuing to work for the benefit of all of the animals.

---

wrong   **milk and apples**   **'Four legs good, two legs bad'**
propaganda   **debates**   **brilliant**   **responsibility**   **Jones**

78

Dr Jekyll and Mr Hyde

Jekyll is a well-respected _____ in London. He is quite well off and likes to throw dinner parties. He has drawn up a _____ which, if he dies or disappears, will leave all of his wealth to Hyde. Utterson, Jekyll's _____, is very worried about this will. Jekyll is interested in the idea that people have a good side and an _____ side. When he carries out experiments into this theory he creates a potion that changes his personality. He turns into a man called _____, who has all of Jekyll's worst traits and is completely evil with no feelings of _____ While Jekyll is transformed into Hyde he brutally knocks down a young girl and stamps on her, and then kills _____ At the start Jekyll could choose when to return into his own self. However, over time Jekyll loses this ability and changes into Hyde even when he does not want to. Finally, he finds that he cannot return to his own self when he wants to. Because of this he eventually _____ We learn about his story because he leaves a confession for _____ to read.

will   evil   Hyde   lawyer   commits suicide   doctor
Utterson   Sir Danvers Carew   guilt

2 Write four personality traits of Squealer (*Animal Farm*) or Dr Jekyll (*Dr Jekyll and Mr Hyde*) in the table below and give examples from the text (for example, an event or a piece of dialogue) to back them up.

	Personality trait	Evidence from the text
1		
2		
3		
4		

Activity 2

15 MINS

In the examination, when you write about what you learn of a character within an extract, you need to give evidence from the extract to support what you have said. This is important if you want to get a good mark.

1 Read the extract relevant to the text you have studied. Then complete the table about **either** Squealer **or** Utterson. This activity will help you to show your knowledge of a character using evidence from the text.

Animal Farm, Chapter 5, page 35

> Afterwards Squealer was sent round the farm to explain the new arrangement to the others.
>
> 'Comrades,' he said, 'I trust that every animal here appreciates the sacrifice that Comrade Napoleon has made in taking this extra labour upon himself. Do not imagine, comrade, that leadership is a pleasure! On the contrary, it is a deep and heavy responsibility. No one believes more firmly than Comrade Napoleon that all animals are equal. He would be only too happy to let you make your decisions for yourselves. But sometimes you might make the wrong decisions, comrades, and then where should we be? Suppose you had decided to follow Snowball, with his moonshine of windmills – Snowball, who, as we now know, was no better than a criminal?'
>
> 'He fought bravely at the Battle of the Cowshed,' said somebody.
>
> 'Bravery is not enough,' said Squealer. 'Loyalty and obedience are more important. And as to the Battle of the Cowshed, I believe the time will come when we shall find that Snowball's part in it was much exaggerated. Discipline, comrades, iron discipline! That is the watchword for today. One false step, and our enemies would be upon us. Surely, comrades, you do not want Jones back?'

What we know about the character, Squealer	Evidence
	Afterwards Squealer was sent round the farm to explain the new arrangement to the others.
	'Comrades,' he said, 'I trust that every animal here appreciates the sacrifice that Comrade Napoleon has made'
With this exclamation, Squealer is making the other animals think that they are lucky to have Napoleon as a leader because it is a hard job – again a sign of this deception.	'Do not imagine, Comrades, that leadership is a pleasure!'
	'Snowball, who, as we now know, was no better than a criminal?'
	'Bravery is not enough,' said Squealer.

Dr Jekyll and Mr Hyde, 'Search for Mr Hyde', page 14

From that time forward, Mr Utterson began to haunt the door in the bystreet of shops. In the morning before office hours, at noon when business was plenty and time scarce, at night under the face of the fogged city moon, by all lights and at all hours of solitude or concourse, the lawyer was to be found on his chosen post.

'If he be Mr Hyde,' he had thought, 'I shall be Mr Seek'.

And at last his patience was rewarded. It was a fine dry night; frost in the air; the streets as clean as a ballroom floor; the lamps, unshaken by any wind, drawing a regular pattern of light and shadow. By ten o'clock, when the shops were closed, the bystreet was very solitary and, in spite of the low growl of London from all round, very silent. Small sounds carried far; domestic sounds out of the houses were clearly audible on either side of the roadway; and the rumour of the approach of any passenger preceded him by a long time. Mr Utterson had been some minutes at his post, when he was aware of an odd, light footstep drawing near. In the course of his nightly patrols, he had long grown accustomed to the quaint effect with which the footfalls of a single person, while he is still a great way off, suddenly spring out distinct from the vast hum and clatter of the city. Yet his attention had never before been so sharply and decisively arrested; and it was with a strong, superstitious prevision of success that he withdrew into the entry of the court.

What we know about the character, Utterson	Evidence
The verb 'haunt' suggests Utterson is a mysterious character	Mr Utterson began to haunt the door in the bystreet of shops
	by all lights and at all hours of solitude or concourse, the lawyer was to be found on his chosen post.
	And at last his patience was rewarded.
	Yet his attention had never before been so sharply and decisively arrested;
	it was with a strong, superstitious prevision of success that he withdrew into the entry of the court.

Activity 3

25 MINS

1 In Activity 2 your judgements about the character were based on an extract that told you something about the way they behaved. In this activity you are asked to respond to an extract in which a character is described by the author. Answer the questions about the extract from the text you have studied below to help you think about how the character is presented. Remember that you will not get these types of questions on the extract in your examination.

Animal Farm, Chapter 4, pages 25–26

> But once again the men, with their sticks and their hobnailed boots, were too strong for them; and suddenly, at a squeal from Snowball, which was the signal for retreat, all the animals turned and fled through the gateway into the yard. The men gave a shout of triumph. They saw, as they imagined, their enemies in flight, and they rushed after them in disorder. This was just what Snowball had intended. As soon as they were well inside the yard, the three horses, the three cows and the rest of the pigs, who had been lying in ambush in the cowshed, suddenly emerged in their rear, cutting them off. Snowball now gave the signal for the charge. He himself dashed straight for Jones.

a What can you learn about Snowball from the phrase 'at a squeal from Snowball, which was the signal for retreat'?

b What does the sentence 'This was just what Snowball had intended' tell us about Snowball?

c When the animals charged, Snowball 'himself dashed straight for Jones.' Does this tell us anything about Snowball?

Dr Jekyll and Mr Hyde, 'Story of the Door', page 5

Mr Utterson the lawyer was a man of a rugged countenance, that was never lighted by a smile; cold, scanty and embarrassed in discourse; backward in sentiment; lean, long, dusty, dreary, and yet somehow lovable. At friendly meetings, and when the wine was to his taste, something eminently human beaconed from his eye; something indeed which never found its way into his talk, but which spoke not only in these silent symbols of the after-dinner face, but more often and loudly in the acts of his life. He was austere with himself; drank gin when he was alone, to mortify a taste for vintages; and though he enjoyed the theatre, had not crossed the doors of one for twenty years. But he had an approved tolerance for others; sometimes wondering almost with envy, at the high pressure of spirits involved in their misdeeds; and in any extremity inclined to help rather than to reprove.

a This is the first thing we are told about Mr Utterson: 'Mr Utterson the lawyer was a man of a rugged countenance, that was never lighted by a smile'. What does the author want us to think about Utterson from this information?

_____

_____

b We are told that Utterson is 'lean, long, dusty, dreary, and yet somehow lovable'. What does this suggest about him?

_____

_____

c We are told that 'He was austere with himself; drank gin when he was alone, to mortify a taste for vintages.' What might this tell us about his character?

_____

_____

Build better answers

1 In this activity you will assess a student's work. Read the sample examination question then look at the relevant extract on page 80 or 81 and read the student's answer.

15 MINS

Animal Farm

From this extract, what do you learn about the character of Squealer? Use evidence from the extract to support your answer. **(8 marks)**

We can see that Squealer is controlled by Napoleon because he 'was sent' round the farm. However, he pretends that he one is of the farm animals by referring to them as 'Comrades'. Squealer's job is to persuade the animals that they are lucky to have Napoleon in control. He is a persuasive talker and is good at twisting the truth. For example, he says that leadership is not a pleasure but 'a deep and heavy responsibility' implying that Napoleon does not enjoy his position. We understand that Napoleon makes decisions to suit himself, but Squealer says that he makes all of the decisions because the animals 'might make the wrong decisions.' This suggests that Napoleon is doing them a favour by acting as a dictator.

Dr Jekyll and Mr Hyde

From this extract, what do you learn about the character of Utterson? Use evidence from the extract to support your answer. **(8 marks)**

Utterson seems to be a mysterious person, as he 'began to haunt the doorway' like a ghost. However, he has taken the job of finding Hyde very seriously. The use of the phrase 'his chosen post' suggests that he sees it as a job. We learn that he is a patient man because 'his patience was rewarded.' Although he has been waiting for days, when he does see Hyde he becomes completely alert as 'his attention had never before been so sharply and decisively arrested.' This shows how keen he was to meet Hyde. Utterson's keenness to see Hyde can be seen because when he heard the noise of Hyde approaching he had a 'strong superstitious prevision of success.'

2 Using the mark scheme below say which band you think the student's answer best fits into. Explain your reasons.

The student's answer would achieve a Band _____ because _____

_____

_____

3 Using your knowledge of the mark scheme, write a short PEE (point, evidence and explanation) paragraph to explain one thing we learn about either Snowball (*Animal Farm*) or Mr Utterson (*Dr Jekyll and Mr Hyde*) from the extract on page 82 or 83. Aim to meet both the Band 3 criteria.

_____

_____

_____

_____

_____

Band	Description
1	• Basic or limited understanding of the character • Uses unclear and/or limited evidence from the extract to demonstrate knowledge about the character
2	• Shows occasional understanding of the character • Uses mostly relevant evidence from the extract to demonstrate knowledge about the character
3	• Generally sound or sound understanding of the character • Uses relevant evidence from the extract to demonstrate knowledge about the character

ResultsPlus
Build your skills

Fill in the RAG table below to see how your confidence has improved in the following areas:

	R	A	G
I can show that I have a sound understanding of characters	○	○	○
I can pick out examples from the text and explain how these show the reader something about a character	○	○	○

3 Exploring a relationship, theme, event, idea or setting

I need to:

- **explain how the writer presents a relationship, theme, event, idea or setting**
- **comment on the writer's use of language**
- **give relevant examples from the extract to support my points.**

In **part (b)** of Section A of the examination you will be asked to look at the same extract you used to answer parts (a) and (c). You will be asked to explain how the writer presents a relationship, a theme, an event, an idea or a setting within this extract.

In **part (d)** of Section A you will be asked to explain how the writer presents a similar relationship, theme, event, idea or setting in **one other** part of the text you have studied. You will need to choose this extract yourself.

ResultsPlus
Build your skills

Fill in the RAG table below to show how confident you are in the following areas:

	R	A	G
I can explain how the writer presents a relationship, theme, event, idea or setting in an extract from the text	○	○	○
I can comment on specific language features and explain their effect	○	○	○
I can give relevant examples from the extract to support my points	○	○	○

Activity 1

7 MINS

Below are some examples of the types of questions you may be asked in parts (b) and/or (d) of Section A of the examination. You will need to have a good general understanding of the characters, relationships, events, themes, ideas and settings within the text you have studied in order to explain how these are presented within an extract.

> Explore how the writer presents the theme of… in the extract/one other part of the novel

> Explain how the writer presents the setting of… in the extract/one other part of the novel

> Explain how the character of… is presented in the extract/one other part of the novel

> Explain how the writer presents the actions of… in the extract/one other part of the novel

> Explain how the relationship between… is presented in the extract/one other part of the novel

> Explain how the writer presents the attitudes of… in the extract/one other part of the novel

> Explain how the writer creates an impression of… in the extract/one other part of the novel

This activity will help you to revise your knowledge about one of the themes from the text you have studied and to practise using evidence to support the points you make about how the theme is presented within an extract.

1   Look at the extract from your text which is specified below. Then match up the pieces of evidence from the extract (the boxes on the left) with the statements that explain what the evidence tells us about the theme of trust (*Animal Farm*), or friendship (*Dr Jekyll and Mr Hyde*).

Animal Farm, Chapter 5, page 35

Read the section of text in Chapter 5, page 35 starting '"Comrades," he said, I trust...' and finishing at '"I will work harder"'.

Evidence	What the evidence tells us about the theme of trust
'Comrades', he said	Squealer dismisses Snowball and makes him seem ridiculous with this abstract description of him. This implies that they should trust Napoleon instead.
'...in taking this extra labour upon himself'	The use of this familiar term of address by Squealer, which is used frequently, makes the animals feel as though they are close friends with Squealer which helps him to influence them. He is asking them to trust him so that he can lie to them.
'Snowball, with his moonshine of windmills'	By using this noun to describe leadership, which suggests hardship and suffering rather than enjoyment, Squealer is trying to make Napoleon seem selfless and make the animals feel grateful and trust him.
'I believe the time will come when we shall find that Snowball's part in it was much exaggerated'	Squealer uses a powerful, moving phrase to start this sentence to try to encourage the animals to share his beliefs. The animals are encouraged to trust Squealer's account of the events even though they are false.

Dr Jekyll and Mr Hyde, 'Dr Jekyll was Quite at Ease', pages 19–20

Read the section of text in Dr Jekyll and Mr Hyde, from 'Dr Jekyll was Quite at Ease', pages 19 – 20 starting 'The large handsome face of Dr Jekyll...' and finishing at '"Well," said he. "I promise."'

Evidence	What the evidence tells us about the theme of friendship
'you know me: I am a man to be trusted'	The use of this first word shows that Utterson has doubts about doing what his friend asks (Utterson does not like Mr Hyde) but does it anyway because the friendship between Utterson and Dr Jekyll is strong.
'My good Utterson'	Jekyll uses exaggeration and a colloquial word in this phrase to emphasise his trust of his friend Utterson
'I would trust you before any man alive, ay, before myself...'	Jekyll addresses his friend in a familiar way which conveys his affection and gratitude
'Well,' said he. 'I promise'.	Utterson uses personal pronouns to make a direct reference to their friendship and knowledge of each other's characters in trying to persuade his friend to tell him about his problem with My Hyde.

Activity 2

15 MINS

In this activity you will look at the writer's use of language in presenting either the theme of power (*Animal Farm*) or the setting of London (*Dr Jekyll and Mr Hyde*).

1 Read the passage below from the text that you have studied, and then answer the questions that follow.

Animal Farm, Chapter 5, pages 33–34

> By the time he had finished speaking there was no doubt as to which way the vote would go. But just at this moment Napoleon stood up, casting a peculiar sidelong look at Snowball, uttered a high-pitched whimper of a kind no one had ever heard him utter before.
>
> At this there was a terrible baying sound outside, and nine enormous dogs wearing brass-studded collars came bounding into the barn. They dashed straight for Snowball, who only sprang from his place just in time to escape their snapping jaws. In a moment he was out of the door and they were after him. Too amazed and frightened to speak, all the animals crowded through the door to watch the chase. Snowball was racing across the long pasture that led to the road. He was running as only a pig can run, but the dogs were close on his heels. Suddenly he slipped and it seemed certain that they had him. Then he was up again, running faster than ever, then the dogs were gaining on him again. One of them all but closed his jaws on Snowball's tail, but Snowball whisked it free just in time. Then he put on an extra spurt and, with a few inches to spare, slipped through a hole in the hedge and was seen no more.

a What is suggested about Napoleon in the phrase he 'uttered a high-pitched whimper of a kind no one had ever heard him utter before'?

_____

_____

b What impression do you get of the dogs from the information that they had 'brass-studded collars' and had 'snapping jaws'?

_____

_____

c How do you think Orwell wants us to respond to Snowball when we are told that 'Suddenly he slipped and it seemed certain that they had him'?

_____

_____

Dr Jekyll and Mr Hyde, 'Search for Mr Hyde', page 14

By ten o'clock, when the shops were closed, the by-street was very solitary and, in spite of the low growl of London from all round, very silent. Small sounds carried far; domestic sounds out of the houses were clearly audible on either side of the roadway; and the rumour of the approach of any passenger preceded him by a long time. Mr Utterson had been some minutes at his post, when he was aware of an odd, light footstep drawing near. In the course of his nightly patrols, he had long grown accustomed to the quaint effect with which the footfalls of a single person, while he is still a great way off, suddenly spring out distinct from the vast hum and clatter of the city. Yet his attention had never before been so sharply and decisively arrested; and it was with a strong, superstitious prevision of success that he withdrew into the entry of the court.

a What atmosphere is suggested by the phrase 'the by-street was very solitary'?

_____

_____

b What does the phrase 'the low growl of London' suggest about London?

_____

_____

c What does the phrase 'the rumour of the approach of any passenger' add to the atmosphere of this extract?

_____

_____

Activity 3

25 MINS

1 Part (d) of the examination question asks you to write about the way a relationship, a theme, an event, an idea or a setting is presented in a different extract from the text. You will need to choose this extract yourself.

a Read the question below, relating to the text you have studied. Find a suitable extract from the text which you could use in response to the question.

Animal Farm

The writer explores the theme of fear in the extract on page 88. Explain how Orwell presents the theme of fear in **one other** part of *Animal Farm*.

Use examples of the writer's language to support your answer. **(12 marks)**

Dr Jekyll and Mr Hyde

The writer explores the theme of suspense in the extract on page 89. Explain how Stevenson presents this theme in **one other** part of the novel.

Use examples of the writer's language to support your answer. **(12 marks)**

b Now list three examples of language that you can write about in your response. Note down how they present the theme by completing the table below.

Extract (chapter and page): _____

Brief description of what happens in the extract:

_____

	Example of language	How it presents the theme
1		
2		
3		

2 Now write a response to the sample part (d) question opposite using the extract you have chosen and the examples of language you have already identified.

Build better answers

13 MINS In this activity you will assess an extract from a student's work. The student has been asked to answer a part (b) sample examination question, explaining how the writer presents a theme in a specific extract.

1 Re-read the relevant extract in Activity 2 on pages 88 – 89 and then read the student's answer to the questions given.

Animal Farm

> Explain how the writer presents fear in the extract.
> Use examples of the writer's language from the extract. **(10 marks)**

Orwell makes it clear that the animals are frightened. First of all we are told that there was a 'terrible baying sound outside' before nine 'enormous' dogs came in wearing 'brass studded collars'. Orwell leaves it up to the reader to imagine how frightened the animals would have been by the sounds and the images that they experienced. Up until this moment there had been a sense that all the animals were working together, even when Snowball and Napoleon disagreed, so this violence would have been frightening. We realise directly how frightened the animals were when we are told that they were 'too amazed and frightened to speak' after Snowball had been chased out of the barn. They were speechless because of their fear.

Dr Jekyll and Mr Hyde

> Explain how the writer presents suspense in the extract.
> Use examples of the writer's language from the extract. **(10 marks)**

This atmosphere in this passage is tense and threatening. We know that there are not many people around because 'the shops are closed' and the place where Utterson is waiting is 'solitary' so we feel that he might be in danger. London also seems threatening — the 'low growl' of the city suggests that the author is comparing it to a wild animal or maybe a monster. The tension builds as we hear Hyde approaching. We first learn that Utterson can hear even the 'rumour' of someone approaching. The word rumour suggests mystery and uncertainty. Later we hear the 'odd, light footstep' drawing near. The word odd suggests that it is not a normal person who approaches, and the fact that Utterson hears the footstep from a long way away suggests that we will have to wait to find out who it is, increasing the suspense and tension.

2 Using the mark scheme below, decide which band the student's answer would achieve and explain the reasons for your decision.

I think the student would achieve Band _____ because _____

_____

_____

_____

_____

Band	Description
3	• Some reference to how the writer achieves effects • Occasional understanding of linguistic, grammatical, structural and presentational features of language • Examples from the extract are occasionally relevant
4	• Generally sound reference to how the writer achieves effects • Generally sound understanding of linguistic, grammatical, structural and presentational features of language • Examples from the extract are generally sound and mostly relevant
5	• Sound reference to how the writer to achieves effects • Clear understanding of linguistic, grammatical, structural and presentational features of language • Examples from the extract are sound and mostly relevant

Fill in the RAG table below to see how your confidence has improved in the following areas:

	R	A	G
I can explain how the writer presents a relationship, theme, event, idea or setting in an extract from the text	○	○	○
I can comment on specific language features and explain their effect	○	○	○
I can give relevant examples from the extract to support my points	○	○	○

4 Responding to an essay question

I need to:

- **respond to the character, relationship, theme, event, idea or setting asked for in the question.**
- **select appropriate details from the text to support my ideas**
- **comment on these details from the text.**

This lesson and Lesson 5 will help you to practise answering the single essay question you will be given for Section B of the examination. This question will ask you about a character, relationship, event, theme, idea or setting within the text you have studied. You will be given three bullet points to give you guidance on what you should cover in your response. Within your answer, you will need to show some awareness of the context of the text you have studied. This will be covered in Lesson 5.

ResultsPlus
Build your skills

Fill in the RAG table below to show how confident you are in the following areas:

	R	A	G
I can respond to the characters, relationships, events, ideas and settings in the text	○	○	○
I can select appropriate details from the text to support my ideas	○	○	○
I can comment on these details	○	○	○

Activity 1

10 MINS

This activity will help to remind you about some of the ideas on character, relationships and themes within the text you have studied.

1 Look at the table relating to your chosen text. Who do you think each of the statements refers to? Choose from the options in the box.

Of Mice and Men

George	Crooks	Curley's wife

✎	Character	Statement
		...tells his friend about the dream to keep him happy.
		...has to keep finding his friend jobs.
		...has to sleep in the barn away from the other men.
		...is told by Curley's wife that she could have him lynched.
		... has dreams about starring in films.
		...is not even given a name in the novel.

To Kill a Mockingbird

| Atticus | Scout | Aunt Alexandra |

✏️	Character	Statement
		...is old-fashioned.
		...does not treat Calpurnia as one of the family.
		...learns about racism and how to oppose it.
		...learns not to be prejudiced against Boo Radley.
		...helps the children learn right from wrong.
		...defends Tom because it is the right thing to do, even though it makes him unpopular.
		...discusses difficult issues with the children.

Activity 2

20 MINS

1   Read the extract from your chosen text. Imagine that you have selected the highlighted details to help you answer the essay question. What could you say about each of the highlighted phrases? Write your answers in the table below. Remember that you won't be given an extract in the examination.

Of Mice and Men, Section 1, page 15

Explain the importance of George and Lennie's friendship in the novel.

In your answer you **must** consider:

• how George and Lennie became friends
• why George and Lennie are together
• their dream to own their own land.

You may include other ideas of your own.

Use **evidence** to support your answer.   (40 marks)

George went on. 'With us it ain't like that. **We got a future.** We got somebody to talk to that gives a damn about us. We don't have to sit in no bar room blowin' in our jack jus' because we got no place else to go. **If them other guys gets in jail they can rot for all anybody gives a damn.** But not us.'

Lennie broke in. *'But not us! An' why? Because ….because I got you to look after me, and you got me to look after you, and that's why.'* **He laughed delightedly.** 'Go on now, George!'

'**You got it by heart.** You can do it yourself.'

'No, you. I forget some a' the things. Tell about how it's gonna be.'

Evidence from the text	Your comment
'We got a future.'	George means that he and Lennie have things to look forward to because of their friendship. This sentence also shows how different they are from the other workers on the ranch.
'If them other guys gets in jail they can rot for all anybody gives a damn.'	
'He laughed delightedly.'	
'You got it by heart.'	

How is Scout's family life presented in the novel?

In your answer you **must** consider:

- the words and actions of the family members
- the importance of the Finch family in Maycomb
- attitudes towards the Finch family.

You may include other ideas of your own.

Use **evidence** to support your answer. (40 marks)

Cecil Jacobs [...] had announced in the schoolyard the day before that Scout Finch's daddy defended niggers. I denied it, but told Jem.

'What'd he mean sayin' that?' I asked.

'Nothing,' Jem said. 'Ask Atticus, he'll tell you.'

'Do you defend niggers, Atticus?' I asked him that evening.

'Of course I do. Don't say nigger, Scout. That's common.'

''s what everybody at school says.'

'From now on it'll be everybody less one–'

Evidence from the text	Your comment
'Ask Atticus, he'll tell you.'	Jem doesn't want to explain that Atticus is defending Tom Robinson. However, he knows that Atticus will always explain things to the children, even if it is a difficult subject.
'Don't say nigger, Scout. That's common.'	
''s what everybody at school says.'	
'From now on it'll be everybody less one–'	

2 What else could you write about in your answer to this question? Choose another section of the text and pick out one example to write about. Briefly write notes on a separate sheet of paper to explain what this evidence shows us about **either** George and Lennie's friendship **or** Scout's family life.

Activity 3

20 MINS

1 Look at the sample examination question for your chosen text. Make notes on each of the bullet points to help you plan your answer.

Of Mice and Men

Why are anger and violence common themes in the novel?

In your answer you must consider:

- the reasons why individual characters are angry
- incidents of violence in the novel
- how characters survive their difficult lives.

You may include other ideas of your own.

Use **evidence** to support your answer. (40 marks)

To Kill a Mockingbird

How are honesty and goodness presented through the character of Atticus?

In your answer you must consider:

- the words and actions of Atticus during the trial of Tom Robinson
- how other characters in the novel repay Atticus for his goodness
- Atticus's honesty with his children, Jem and Scout.

You may include other ideas of your own.

Use **evidence** to support your answer. (40 marks)

2 Read the extract from your chosen text. Write one paragraph of the answer to your examination question using evidence from the given extract. Then write another paragraph using evidence from elsewhere in the text. Try and ensure you choose a relevant extract, and make sure the evidence you use really supports the points you make.

Of Mice and Men, Section 4, pages 85–86

Candy laid the stump of his wrist on his knee and rubbed it gently with his hand. He said accusingly, 'You gotta husban'. You got no call foolin' aroun' with other guys, causin' trouble.'

The girl flared up. 'Sure I gotta husban'. You all seen him. Swell guy, ain't he? Spends all his time sayin' what he's gonna do to guys he don't like, and he don't like nobody. Think I'm gonna stay in that two-by-four house and listen how Curley's gonna lead with his left twice, and then bring in the ol' right cross?'

To Kill a Mockingbird,
Chapter 20, pages 210–211

'The witnesses for the state, with the exception of the Sheriff of Maycomb County, have presented themselves to you gentlemen, to this court, in the cynical confidence that their testimony would not be doubted, confident that you gentlemen would go along with them on the assumption – the evil assumption – that *all* Negroes lie, that *all* Negroes are basically immoral beings, that *all* Negro men are not to be trusted around our women, an assumption one associates with minds of their calibre.

'Which, gentlemen, we know is in itself a lie as black as Tom Robinson's skin, a lie I do not have to point out to you. You know the truth, and the truth is this: some Negroes lie, some Negroes are immoral, some Negro men are not to be trusted around women – black or white. But this is a truth that applies to the human race and to no particular race of men.'

1 Read the extract from a student's answer to the sample examination question that appeared in Activity 3. Then read the mark scheme opposite. Which band do you think the response would achieve? Explain your reasons.

Of Mice and Men

The most violent person on the ranch is Curley. He is a good boxer and he always wants to be the toughest on the ranch. When he sees Lennie for the first time he looks aggressive. 'His glance was at once calculating and pugnacious.' Pugnacious means aggressive. Candy warns George that Curley hates big guys because he is so short. He is most angry about his wife. He wanted a traditional wife who would stay in the house and do the housework. But Curley's wife is not like that. She wants to meet people and dreams of being an actress. Curley gets worried that his wife is seeing the other men. He accused Slim who gets angry, and then Carlson is rude to Curley. Curley feels embarrassed by this and so he picks on Lennie because he thinks that he can beat Lennie in a fight.

To Kill a Mockingbird

During the trial of Tom Robinson we see the honesty and goodness of Atticus. Even when he showed that Mayella's evidence was false, Scout says 'Atticus had hit her hard in a way that was not clear to me, but it gave him no pleasure at all.' This shows that he felt bad about making Mayella so upset, even though he showed that she was telling lies. When he summed up the evidence he told the jury how racist they were, because they believed 'that all Negroes lie, that all Negroes are basically immoral beings, that all Negro men are not to be trusted around our women.' After the trial, even though Tom Robinson was found guilty, the black people of Maycomb were grateful. 'The kitchen table was loaded with enough food to bury the family.' This shows how grateful the people were, because they were very poor and gave Atticus what they had.

Band	Description
3	• Some responses to text supported by textual reference which is occasionally appropriate • Selection and evaluation of textual detail show some understanding of theme/ideas
4	• Mostly sound responses to text mostly supported by textual reference which is often appropriate • Selection and evaluation of textual detail show generally sound understanding of theme/ideas
5	• Sound responses to text supported by relevant textual reference • Selection and evaluation of textual detail show sound understanding of theme/ideas

 I think this response would achieve Band _____ because _____

_____

Remember that your response to the Section B essay question will be assessed against this mark scheme and the mark scheme on page 109, covering reference to the context of your text, your explanation of the importance of the topic you are writing on, as well as spelling, punctuation and grammar. These will be covered in Lesson 5.

Fill in the RAG table below to see how your confidence has improved in the following areas:

	R	A	G
I can respond to the characters, relationships, events, ideas and settings in the text	○	○	○
I can select appropriate details from the text to support my ideas	○	○	○
I can comment on these details	○	○	○

5 Responding to the context of the text

I need to:

- **show an awareness of the context of the text, following the guidance given in the question**
- **explain the importance of the themes and ideas**
- **structure my sentences and spell and punctuate accurately.**

This lesson will continue to help you prepare for the essay question you will tackle in Section B of the examination. You will be writing about a character, relationship, event, theme, idea or setting, and you will need to show some understanding of the context of your text within your response, e.g. by explaining why Curley's wife behaves as she does on the ranch, or by giving some suggestions as to why Tom Robinson was accused of the rape of Mayella Ewell. You should not give detailed or extensive historical, social or cultural information within your essay.

ResultsPlus
Build your skills

Fill in the RAG table below to show how confident you are in the following areas:

	R	A	G
I can make reference to the text's context, supported by evidence from the text	○	○	○
I can comment on the themes and ideas of the text	○	○	○
I can structure my sentences so the meaning is clear, use a full range of punctuation and spell accurately	○	○	○

Activity 1

15 MINS

1 Read the information about your text to make sure you understand the context. You will not need to give information like this in your essay. Answer the questions which follow to help you to think about how the context is relevant to the characters, themes and events you will write about in your essay.

Of Mice and Men

Of Mice and Men is set during the 1930s depression in America. During this period one in every four men lost their jobs and because prices for farm produce fell enormously, farmers found it difficult to operate. The action in the novel takes place in California where lots of farm labourers like George and Lennie travelled alone from farm to farm looking for work. Jobs often lasted for only a short time and then the workers had to move on to look for more work. Because they travelled alone there were very few friendships.

a In the depression, farm prices fell. Wages also fell and there was no job security. How does this affect the characters in *Of Mice and Men*?

_____

_____

b Most farm jobs only lasted for
a short time on the ranches. How does this affect the characters in the novel?

_____

_____

c In the 1930s it was difficult for women to be independent. How is this shown in the novel?

_____

_____

To Kill a Mockingbird

To Kill a Mockingbird is set during the 1930s in America. Because of the depression many families, both whites and African Americans, were poor. The novel is set in Alabama and focuses on the racism of a small town. Although slavery was abolished in 1865, African Americans were still treated very badly at this time. In the South, there were laws which said that African Americans and white people could not mix. There were separate schools, restaurants and even water fountains. Although the law said that all Americans were equal, in practice, juries almost always believed white people over African Americans.

a The depression of the 1930s meant that a lot of people were very poor. Who is poor in the novel? How does Harper Lee show this?

_____

_____

b African Americans were supposed to be 'separate but equal' to white people in the southern states of the US. Are the African American characters treated in an 'equal' way in the novel? Explain your answer.

_____

_____

c Bob Ewell is one of the most racist characters in the book. Why do you think this is?

_____

_____

Activity 2

1 Look at the sample examination question relevant to the text you have studied on page 106. Then look at the short extract below and answer the questions to help you start thinking about how to respond to the sample examination question. Remember that you will not be given an extract or questions like this in the examination.

15 MINS

Of Mice and Men, Section 2, page 34

> Both men glanced up for the rectangle of sunshine in the doorway was cut off. A girl was standing there looking in. She had full, rouged lips and wide-spaced eyes, heavily made up. Her fingernails were red. Her hair hung in little rolled clusters, like sausages. She wore a cotton house dress and red mules, on the insteps of which were little bouquets of red ostrich feathers. 'I'm lookin' for Curley,' she said. Her voice had a nasal, brittle quality.
>
> George looked away from her and then back. 'He was in here a minute ago, but he went.'
>
> 'Oh!' She put her hands behind her back and leaned against the door frame so that her body was thrown forward. 'You're the new fellas that just come, ain't ya?'
>
> 'Yeah.'
>
> Lennie's eyes moved down over her body, and though she did not seem to be looking at Lennie, she bridled a little. She looked at her fingernails. 'Sometimes Curley's in here,' she explained.

a Why might the ranchers feel that Curley's wife is a 'tart'?

_____

_____

b What is the role of Curley's wife on the ranch? Were there many women on the ranches?

_____

_____

c How do the men respond to Curley's wife's behaviour?

_____

_____

d Why does Curley's wife flirt with the men? Does she really like them?

_____

_____

To Kill a Mockingbird, Chapter 18, pages 187–188

She was looking at him furiously.

'Won't answer a word you say long as you keep on mockin' me,' she said.

'Ma'am?' asked Atticus, startled.

'Long's you keep on makin' fun o'me.'

Judge Taylor said, 'Mr Finch is not making fun of you. What's the matter with you?'

Mayella looked from under lowered eyelids at Atticus, but she said to the judge: 'Long's he keeps on callin' me ma'am an' sayin' Miss Mayella. I don't hafta take his sass, I ain't called upon to take it.'

a Why is Mayella shut out from the white community?

_____

_____

b Why does Mayella think Atticus is making fun of her?

_____

_____

c Tom Robinson says that he called her 'Miss Mayella'. Do you think she thought he was making fun of her too? Why or why not?

_____

_____

d What do most white people in Maycomb think about the Ewells? Why? What does this tell us about Maycomb society?

_____

_____

Activity 3

1 Read the sample examination question for your chosen text. Make notes on each of the bullet points in the question to help you start planning a response. You may want to use the ideas you explored in Activity 2.

Of Mice and Men

Explain the importance of Curley's wife in the novel.

In your answer you must consider:

• the relationship between Curley's wife and Curley

• how the men describe and treat Curley's wife

• the hopes and dreams of Curley's wife. (40 marks)

To Kill a Mockingbird

What is the role of Mayella Ewell in the novel?

In your answer you must consider:

• the events involving Mayella Ewell

• what the events tell the reader about the Ewell family

• the trial of Tom Robinson. (40 marks)

2   Now write at least two paragraphs in response to the sample examination question. If you wish, the first can be focused on the evidence you explored in Activity 2. The second paragraph should use separate pieces of evidence from your text. Remember that you need to make reference to the context of your text wherever this is appropriate to support your points in order to gain good marks. Your writing will also be assessed for spelling, grammar and punctuation.

3   Now check over your response to ensure you have done the following:

• Given evidence from the text to support your answer

• Made reference to the context of the novel wherever this is appropriate to explore the character, relationship, event, theme, idea or setting you are writing about

• Used correct grammar, spelling and punctuation in your writing.

Build better answers

10 MINS

1 Read the extract taken from a student's response to the sample examination question in Activity 3. Then read the mark scheme opposite. This mark scheme will be used to assess your essay in the examination, along with the mark scheme in Lesson 4 on page 101. Decide which band you think the student answer would achieve and explain your reasons. Remember to think about grammar, spelling and punctuation.

Of Mice and Men

At first it seems that Curley's wife is not very significant in the novel because we don't even know her name. However, this just shows that at the time women were not seen as very important. Curley thinks that he owns her and keeps checking where she is. At the start of the novel Candy tells us that she is a 'tart' and when George and Lennie see her she flirts with them. 'She had full, rouged lips and wide-spaced eyes, heavily made up.' This is not right for a ranch. But when she talks to Lennie at the end of the novel we see another side to her. She tells Lennie that she wanted to be an actress and live an exciting life. She also told Lennie that she hated Curley and so she was very lonely on the ranch. We can see that she dressed like she did to look like an actress and she was always trying to talk to the ranchers because she was lonely. She was not anything like a 'tart'.

To Kill a Mockingbird

Mayella Ewell lives with her family behind the town garbage dump in a run-down house. They are very poor as Bob Ewell is nearly always unemployed. The novel is set in the 1930s depression in America so it is not surprising that he finds it difficult to find work. However, whenever he does get money he spends it on alcohol rather than his family. Mayella Ewell tries to make the 'dirty' yard look nice by planting 'bright red geraniums'. Mayella is really lonely. We are told that 'white people wouldn't have anything to do with her because she lived amongst pigs' and she is so surprised when Atticus treats her with respect that she thinks he is mocking her. Through Mayella we see that Maycomb society is prejudiced against people like the Ewells as well as racist. However, in the end, the jury are still more prejudiced against Tom because of his colour. They convict Tom, even though Mayella and Bob are clearly lying. This shows that people in that society were often so racist that they will believe any white person over any black person, even if the white person is a liar and the black person is honest.

Band	Description
3	• Some reference to context occasionally supported by relevant textual reference • Explanation of importance of theme/idea in the extract shows occasional understanding • Sentences show some attempt to structure and control expression and meaning with some control of a range of punctuation devices. Spelling sometimes accurate with meaning hindered on occasion
4	• Mostly sound reference to context mostly supported by relevant textual reference • Explanation of importance of theme/idea shows generally sound understanding • Sentences are generally clearly structured, with generally sound control of expression and meaning with generally sound control of a range of punctuation devices. Spelling is mostly accurate, any errors do not hinder meaning
5	• Sound reference to context supported by relevant textual reference • Explanation of importance of theme/idea shows sound understanding • Sentences are clearly structured, with sound control of expression and meaning with secure control of the full range of punctuation devices. Spelling is mostly accurate, with some errors

The student's answer would obtain a Band _____ because _____

_____

_____

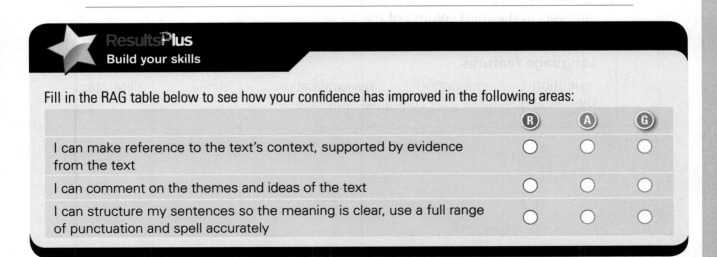

ResultsPlus
Build your skills

Fill in the RAG table below to see how your confidence has improved in the following areas:

	R	A	G
I can make reference to the text's context, supported by evidence from the text	○	○	○
I can comment on the themes and ideas of the text	○	○	○
I can structure my sentences so the meaning is clear, use a full range of punctuation and spell accurately	○	○	○

1 Writing about an unseen poem

I need to:

- **show that I understand what happens in the poem**
- **show that I understand the writer's ideas**
- **explain how the writer uses structure, language and form to present their ideas**
- **give examples from the poem to support my points.**

This lesson will help you to practise answering Section A of the examination for Unit 2 Understanding Poetry.

In Section A you will need to read a poem you have not seen before and explain how the writer uses language, form and structure to present an idea, a theme, or a setting within the poem. You will need to give examples to support your points.

ResultsPlus
Build your skills

Fill in the RAG table below to show how confident you are in the following areas:

	R	A	G
I can recognise a range of poetic devices	○	○	○
I can comment on particular vocabulary	○	○	○
I can comment on the way a poem is organised	○	○	○
I can explain how the writer uses poetic devices, vocabulary and structure to present their ideas	○	○	○

Activity 1

10 MINS

Opposite is a table which contains the definitions of some key language features and poetic devices.

1. Match each of the language features given in the box below to a definition. Write your answers in the first column of the table.

2. Choose an example of each language feature from the box opposite. Write your answers in the third column of the table.

Language features

repetition   metaphor   personification   simile   alliteration
rhetorical question   colloquial language

Examples

He changed me like a glove

We are tidal islands

Well, mate

Do we need it now?

Flicker and fade out from the west

A motorbike snarls;
Dustbins flinch.

Parading round and round and round

	Language feature	Definition	Example
		Asking a question to make a point rather than to get an answer	
		Using words usually found in everyday speech – these can include 'slang' words	
		Comparing two things using a word such as 'like' or 'as'	
		Using at least two words close together that begin with or include the same consonant (letter that is not a vowel)	
		Using the same word or phrase more than once	
		Comparing two things by describing one as something else, without using a word such as 'like'	
		Describing things as if they are human when they are not	

Activity 2

15 MINS

1 Read the short extracts from a range of poems that follow and remind yourself of the poetic devices and language features you identified in Activity 1.

2 For each extract, decide whether the poetic devices highlighted is an example of simile, alliteration, metaphor or personification. Some extracts might be examples of more than one of these devices. Write the poetic devices or language features in the space provided.

3 Comment on ideas or feelings that the poetic devices or language features help to communicate. Write your ideas in the spaces provided.

a

The Warm and the Cold

Freezing dusk is closing
    Like a slow trap of steel
On trees and roads and hills and all
    That can no longer feel.

Ted Hughes

Poetic device/language feature:

_____

_____

Idea or feeling that the language helps to communicate:

_____

_____

b

I am the wind

I am the wisdom and the freedom,
I am the storm that tears and howls,
I am the whispering in the treetops,
I slide beneath you,
swirl around you,
stroke your hair,
and take your breath away.

Anon

Poetic device/language feature:

_____

_____

Extract taken from http://1-poem.com/i_am_the_wind_personification_exercise.htm, 1-poem.com, © copyright Dr Silvia Hartmann, www.1-poem.com

Idea or feeling that the language helps to communicate:

_____

_____

c

The City

In the morning the city
Spreads its wings
Making a song
In stone that sings.

Langston Hughes

Poetic device/language feature:

_____

_____

_____

Idea or feeling that the language helps to communicate:

_____

_____

_____

d

Ode to the West Wind

O wild West Wind, thou breath of
Autumn's being

Percy Bysshe Shelley

Poetic device/language feature:

_____

_____

_____

Idea or feeling that the language helps to communicate:

_____

_____

_____

e

She Walks in Beauty

She walks in beauty, like the night
  Of cloudless climes and starry skies;
And all that's best of dark and bright
  Meet in her aspect and her eyes ...

Lord Byron (George Gordon)

Poetic device/language feature:

_____

_____

_____

Idea or feeling that the language helps to communicate:

_____

_____

_____

When you read a poem that is new to you, it is helpful first to identify the main ideas or feeling of the poem. Once you have done this, you can think about how the writer has used poetic devices, language and structure to get across their ideas.

Activity 3

25 MINS

1 Read the poem below. Briefly answer the following questions:

    a Explain what is described in the poem. What time of the day is it?

_____

    b How does the poem make you feel?

_____

    c What impression does the writer give of the fog?

_____

The Fog

Slowly the fog,
Hunch-shouldered with a grey face,
Arms wide, advances,
Finger-tips touching the way
Past the dark houses
And dark gardens of roses.
Up the short street from the harbour,
Slowly the fog,
Seeking, seeking;
Arms wide, shoulders hunched,
Searching, searching.
Out to the streets, to the fields,
Slowly the fog –
A blind man hunting the moon.

F R McCreary

Extract taken from 'The Fog' by FR McCreary from Opening Eyes: A Poetry Collection, Cambridge
University Press (Phillips, J)

2 Complete the table opposite with at least four examples of language that help to present the main ideas and feelings of the poem. The poetic devices have been named for you. One entry has been completed as an example.

Poetic device or language feature	Example	How this is used to present the writer's ideas, thoughts or feelings
Personification	Hunch-shouldered with a grey face	This gives the idea that the fog is moving like a stooping man, his face old and lacking in colour.
Metaphor		
Repetition		
Alliteration		

3 Write a paragraph on a separate piece of paper in response to the following sample examination question:

> Explain how F R McCreary explores ideas about the fog and its effects.
>
> Write about:
> - what happens in the poem
> - how the writer has organised the poem
> - how the writer uses language to show his ideas.
>
> Use evidence from the poem to support your answer. (20 marks)

Remember that you will have to write your response to the examination question in full, clear sentences. Your response is marked for it spelling, grammar and punctuation as well as its content.

4 Read through your answer carefully, checking for meaning and correct spelling, grammar and punctuation.

Build better answers

10 MINS

1 Read the following student response to the sample examination question from Activity 3. Highlight all the extracts from the poem that the student has included as evidence to support their points.

> In this poem the writer makes a lot of use of personification to describe the fog. It describes the fog as being a man, with an actual body. I think it is an old man because it says 'hunch-shouldered with a grey face'. The fog has a grey face because it makes everything around look grey. The use of 'finger-tips' gives the idea of feeling your way, but also it is like it is touching you with its clammy fingers.
>
> You also get the impression that the fog is slowly coming in from the sea, so it is like someone who has arrived at the harbour and is now crossing the town and going out into the countryside ('through the streets to the fields'). The last line is a metaphor comparing the fog to a blind man looking for the moon, and a blind man cannot see the moon anyway, but now nobody can see it because of the fog.

2 Look at the mark scheme opposite. Decide which band you think the answer would achieve and give reasons for this.

I think the student's answer is in Band _____ because _____

_____

_____

3 Now look back at your own response to the sample examination question that you wrote at the end of Activity 3. Decide which band it would achieve, and then explain how you could improve it.

I think my response would achieve a Band _____

To get into a higher band, I could _____

_____

_____

Band	Description
3	• Some understanding of the poem's content/ideas • Some explanation of how the writer uses language, structure and form to present the poem's content/ideas • Some relevant textual reference to support response • Some control in organising and communicating ideas. Spelling, punctuation and grammar sometimes accurate with meaning hindered on occasion
4	• Generally sound understanding of the poem's content/ideas • Generally sound explanation of how the writer uses language, structure and form to present the poem's content/ideas • Generally sound relevant textual reference to support response • Generally sound organisation and communication of ideas. Spelling, punctuation and grammar is mostly accurate; any errors do not hinder meaning
5	• Sound understanding of the poem's content/ideas • Sound explanation of how the writer uses language, structure and form to present the poem's content/ideas • Sound relevant textual reference to support response • Sound organisation and communication of ideas. Spelling, punctuation and grammar is mostly accurate, with some errors

ResultsPlus
Build your skills

Fill in the RAG table below to see how your confidence has improved in the following areas:

	R	A	G
I can recognise a range of poetic devices	○	○	○
I can comment on particular vocabulary	○	○	○
I can comment on the way a poem is organised	○	○	○
I can explain how the writer uses poetic devices, vocabulary and structure to present their ideas	○	○	○

2 Commenting on one anthology poem

I need to:
- **explain the writer's ideas, thoughts and feelings in the poem**
- **explain how the writer uses language, structure and form to convey these ideas, thoughts and feelings**
- **use relevant examples from the poem to support my points.**

This lesson will help you prepare for the Section B Anthology Poems section of your examination.

You **must** answer part (a).

- **Part (a)** will ask you to comment on the writer's thoughts or feelings in a named poem from your anthology collection.

You should answer **either** part (b)(i) **or** part (b)(ii)

- **Part (b)(i)** will ask you to compare the writer's ideas in the poem from part (a) with another named poem from the same collection in the anthology.

- **Part (b)(ii)** will ask you to compare the writer's ideas in the poem from part (a) with a poem of your choice from the same collection in the anthology.

This lesson focuses on part (a) of the question. This will ask you to describe the writer's thoughts, feelings, ideas or attitudes using examples of language from a named poem in your anthology collection.

ResultsPlus
Build your skills

Fill in the RAG table below to show how confident you are in the following areas:

	R	A	G
I can recognise a range of poetic devices and comment on their effect	○	○	○
I can comment on the effect of particular vocabulary	○	○	○
I can comment on the effect of the structure and form of a poem	○	○	○
I can choose relevant examples from the poem to support my points	○	○	○

Activity 1

10 MINS

Part (a) of the examination question will ask you to write about the writer's ideas, thoughts and feelings in one of the poems you have studied. It is important to know what these key ideas, thoughts and feelings are and how they are presented using language.

1. Choose two poems from your anthology collection. Briefly summarise the main ideas, thoughts and feelings in each poem in the boxes opposite.

2. Writers can use language to present their ideas. For example, they may use simile and metaphor, personification, interesting vocabulary, alliteration, assonance, onomatopoeia, rhythm and rhyme. Remind yourself of the definition of some of these poetic devices if you need to. List some of the techniques the writer uses to present their ideas in each poem you have selected. Record your ideas in the boxes opposite.

Poem 1 _____

Ideas, thoughts or feelings in the poem _____

_____

_____

Techniques used by the poet _____

_____

_____

_____

_____

Poem 2 _____

Ideas, thoughts or feelings in the poem _____

_____

_____

Techniques used by the poet _____

_____

_____

Activity 2

20 MINS

1 Look at the poems in the anthology collection that you have studied. Choose at least six devices that the poets have used to convey their ideas, attitudes, thoughts or feelings. The examples should come from at least two different poems.

2 Complete the table opposite. An example (one from each collection) has been completed for you below.

Poem	Device/feature	Quotation	How this helps the poet to convey ideas, attitudes, thoughts or feelings
Relationships: *Valentine*	Metaphor	'It is a moon wrapped in brown paper'	The poet is suggesting that the gift of an onion is a gift of light, but first it has to be 'unwrapped'. This is compared to 'undressing' but also shows that love is something that is not easy to find.
Clashes and collisions: *Exposure*	Repetition	'But nothing happens'	This short sentence, which is repeated at the end of four stanzas, emphasises how the soldiers can only wait and wait and that nothing is changing.
Somewhere, anywhere: *Orkney/ This Life*	Onomatopoeia	'When a clatter of white whoops and rises…'	The two words 'clatter' and 'whoops' reflect the noises made by the sea bird in the first stanza. However, here they are used to give an impression of the poet and his lover.
Taking a Stand: *Solitude*	Contrast	'Feast, and your halls are crowded;/ Fast and the world goes by'	The contrast of 'feast' and 'fast', with similar sounds but opposite meanings, is an effective way of showing how quickly life can change if you have bad luck, which is the main theme of the poem.

Poem	Device/feature	Quotation	How this helps the poet to convey ideas, attitudes, thoughts or feelings

Activity 3

20 MINS

In this activity you are going to practise planning a response to a sample examination question.

1 Read the question relating to the collection of poems you have studied. Then read the poem. Try to look at a copy of the poem that you have not previously annotated to practise the skills you will need in the examination.

Collection A – Relationships

Describe the writer's thoughts and feelings about relationships between people of different ages in 'Kissing'. (15 marks)

Collection B – Clashes and collisions

Describe the writer's thoughts and feelings about the horror of war in 'The Drum' by John Scott. (15 marks)

Collection C – Somewhere, anywhere

Describe the writer's thoughts and feelings about her mother in 'My Mother's Kitchen' by Choman Hardi. (15 marks)

Collection D – Taking a stand

Describe the writer's thoughts and feelings about how she wishes to be remembered in 'Remember' by Christina Rossetti. (15 marks)

2 The first stage of your plan is to think about the key points you want to make in response to the question. Write down three key points you will make in the table opposite.

3 For each point you make, you must include evidence from the poem. Write down one example from the poem that you will use to support your point. In the examination, you may wish to use more examples, if appropriate.

4 Now write a brief explanation of how the example you have given supports your point. This part is important in order to gain a good mark.

An example for each collection has been completed for you.

Point	Evidence	Explanation
It is not only the young who can feel powerful physical attraction	'Their mouths and tongues are soft and powerful and as moist as ever'	The writer's choice of words shows that middle-aged people can also kiss each other passionately.
War has terrible effects on those left behind, not only the soldiers	'And widows' tears, and orphans' moans'	The writer uses the words 'tears' and 'moans' to refer to the feelings of women and children whose husbands have been killed at war.
Even when she is getting on in years, her mother can still feel excitement about the idea of moving house yet again	'At 69 she is excited about/starting from scratch'	The words 'starting from scratch' emphasise that she is not just having to move, but that she cannot take her possessions with her.
She realises that death will take her a long way from her loved one	'Gone far away into the silent land'	She feels that death will be a complete separation. The phrase 'silent land' shows that she will be unable to communicate with her lover after she has gone.

Build better answers

10 MINS

1 Look closely at the extract below from a student answer to the question on your chosen collection that you planned a response to in Activity 3.

Ask yourself:

- Has the student made an interesting, relevant point?
- Have they given evidence from the poem to support their point?
- Have they explained how the evidence supports their point?

Use a highlighter or underline the **point**, the quotation (**evidence**) and the **explanation** (PEE). Annotate the sample answer with notes about how well the points have been made and supported.

2 Use the mark scheme opposite to decide which band you think the answer would achieve. Write a brief comment explaining your reasons and suggest how the answer could be improved.

Relationships

The poet is saying that people can be in love not only when they are young but also middle-aged people. She shows them in different places kissing. The young people are 'walking on the riverbank'. This shows that they can enjoy each other's company out in the open. But the older people are seen kissing 'in the back of taxis'. It seems as if they have not got long together and have to take their chances where they can.

Clashes and collisions

The two stanzas focus on different aspects of war, though both start with the same lines 'I hate that drum's discordant sound,/Parading round, and round, and round'. This repetition shows how strongly the poet dislikes war. There is alliteration in 'drum's discordant sound', so you can hear the drumming. The parade going 'round, and round, and round' is effective, as if the soldiers are not getting anywhere, like being in a fairground, on a roundabout that never stops. The first stanza shows the attitudes of the soldiers, who are prepared to 'sell their liberty for charms'. This shows the excitement of going to war. They don't realise they might lose their freedom or even their lives, as it says 'To march, and fight, and fall'.

Somewhere, anywhere

At the start and end of the poem Choman Hardi uses repetition to make a contrast. She begins 'I will inherit my mother's kitchen', but at the end she realises that she will never be able to inherit her 'mother's trees'. The things from the kitchen are the only objects that her mother has been able to take with her. She does not worry about having to get new furniture. But the vines and trees are permanent. She cannot take them with her, so her daughter will not inherit them. I think Choman really admires her mother because she can get excited about moving to start a new life.

In 'Remember' Christina Rossetti thinks about what it will be like for her lover after she has gone 'into the silent land'. This shows that when she dies, she realises they will never be able to talk to each other again. She is also being very practical, because she says 'no more day by day you tell me of our future that you planned'. This shows that the lover has been planning for them to have a future together, but that he will have to accept that this cannot be.

Band	Description
3	• Some explanation of how the writer conveys his thoughts and feelings to create effect • Some relevant connection made between thoughts and feelings and the presentation of ideas • Occasional relevent textual reference to support response.
4	• Generally sound explanation of how the writer conveys his thoughts and feelings to create effect. • Generally sound relevant connection made between thoughts and feelings and the presentation of ideas • Mostly clear, relevant textual reference to support their response
5	• Sound explanation of how the writer uses thoughts and feelings to create effect • Sound relevant connection made between thoughts and feelings and the presentation of ideas • Clear, relevant textual reference to support response.

ResultsPlus
Build your skills

Fill in the RAG table below to see how your confidence has improved in the following areas:

	R	A	G
I can recognise a range of poetic devices and comment on their effect	○	○	○
I can comment on the effect of particular vocabulary	○	○	○
I can comment on the effect of the structure and form of a poem	○	○	○
I can choose relevant examples from the poem to support my points	○	○	○

3 Comparing two poems

I need to:

- make comparisons and links between the poems
- compare the ways the two poets present their ideas
- use relevant quotations to support my ideas.

This lesson will help you prepare for the Section B Anthology Poems section of your examination. This lesson focuses on **part (b)** of the question. This will ask you to compare the way two writers present their ideas about the same theme.

You should answer **either** part (b)(i) **or** part (b)(ii).

- Part (b)(i) will ask you to compare the writer's ideas in the poem from part (a) with another named poem from the anthology collection you have studied.

- Part (b)(ii) will ask you to compare the writer's ideas in the poem from part (a) with a poem of your choice from the anthology collection you have studied.

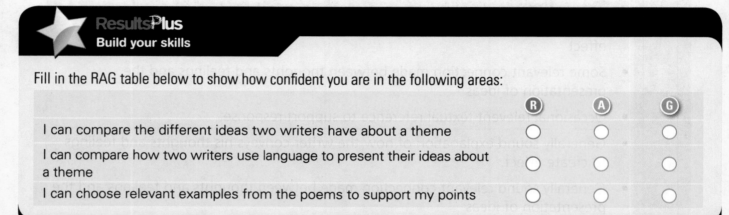

ResultsPlus
Build your skills

Fill in the RAG table below to show how confident you are in the following areas:

	R	A	G
I can compare the different ideas two writers have about a theme	○	○	○
I can compare how two writers use language to present their ideas about a theme	○	○	○
I can choose relevant examples from the poems to support my points	○	○	○

Activity 1

10 MINS

In part (b) of the examination, you will need to compare how writers present their thoughts, feelings, ideas or attitudes. Before you go into the examination, it is important to have a good understanding of the main themes, ideas and feelings in the poems you have studied.

1 Look at the following words which describe key feelings. Decide which are 'positive' and which 'negative' and put a P or N in the next column.

2 Fill in the columns of the table for at least four of the key words, showing similar words, words with the opposite meaning and poems from your anthology collection that present these feelings.

Key words to describe people's feelings	Positive or negative?	Word with similar meaning	Poem which contains this feeling	Word with opposite meaning	Poem which contains this feeling
bitter					
frustrated					
tender					
disappointed					
excited					
passionate					
loving					
irritated					
affectionate					
hostile					

Activity 2

15 MINS

When you are comparing two poems, you are looking for things that are similar in the poets' ideas or approach as well as things that are different.

1 Look at quotations from two poems in the anthology collection that you have studied.

Relationships

Sonnet 116

'Love's not Time's fool, though rosy lips and cheeks
Within his bending sickle's compass come;'

One Flesh

'And time itself's a feather
Touching them gently. Do they know they're old,
These two who are my father and my mother
Whose fire from which I came, has now grown cold?'

Clashes and collisions

The Drum

'I hate that drum's discordant sound,
Parading round, and round, and round'

O What is that Sound

'O what is that sound which so thrills the ear
Down in the valley drumming, drumming?'

Somewhere, anywhere

Cape Town Morning

'And trucks digest the city's sediment
men gloved and silent
in the municipal jaws'

Composed upon Westminster Bridge, September 3, 1802

'This City now doth, like a garment, wear
The beauty of the morning; silent, bare'

Taking a stand

Zero Hour

'How long before the shelves are empty
in the supermarkets? The first riots
are raging as I write, and who
out there could have predicted
this sudden countdown to zero hour'

One World Down the Drain

'The millions who will suffer from
Drought, famine and disease.
The weather map is changing
But what are we to do?'

2 Write down the main theme or subject of each quotation and the feelings the writer expresses.

Quotation 1

Main theme/idea _____

The feelings expressed in this quotation _____

_____

Quotation 2

Main theme/idea _____

The feelings expressed in this quotation _____

_____

3 Now decide whether the ideas and feelings expressed in the two quotations are similar, different, or partly similar and partly different, then explain the reasons for your decision in the space below.

I think the ideas expressed in these two quotations are (tick the one you think applies):

Similar ☐   Different ☐   Partly similar and partly different ☐

My reasons:

_____

_____

_____

Activity 3

20 MINS

In this activity you will practise planning an answer to a part (b)(ii) question.

1 Look at the question relating to the anthology collection you have been studying. One of the poems has been chosen for you.

Collection A – Relationships

Explain how the writer of **one** poem of your choice from the 'Relationships' collection presents different ideas about family relationships from those given in 'The Habit of Light'.

Use **evidence** from the poems to support your answer.   (15 marks)

Collection B – Clashes and collisions

Explain how the writer of **one** poem of your choice from the 'Clashes and Collisions' collection presents different ideas about misunderstandings or conflicts between people from those given in 'Your Dad Did What?'.

Use **evidence** from the poems to support your answer.   (15 marks)

Collection C – Somewhere, anywhere

Explain how the writer of **one** poem of your choice from the 'Somewhere, Anywhere' collection presents different thoughts and feelings about a place from those given in 'City Jungle'.

Use **evidence** from the poems to support your answer.   (15 marks)

Collection D – Taking a stand

Explain how the writer of **one** poem of your choice from the 'Take a stand' collection presents different attitudes to life from those given in 'Pessimism for Beginners'.

Use **evidence** from the poems to support your answer.   (15 marks)

2 Choose a suitable poem to compare with the poem named in the question. You need to be able to make useful comparisons between the two poems, showing how they present different ideas. Don't just pick a poem at random!

Chosen poem: _____

_____

3 Now think about the key comparisons you want to make in response to the question. Write the key comparisons in the table below.

4 For each comparison you make, you must include evidence from the poems. In the table, add examples of evidence from each poem that you will use to support your point. In the examination, you may wish to use more examples, if appropriate.

5 Write a brief explanation in the table of how the evidence you have given supports your comparison.

Point (comparison)	Evidence (Poem 1)	Evidence (Poem 2)	Explanation

Build better answers

15 MINS

1 Look at the mark scheme opposite. To get good marks, it is important to know what you are aiming to do.

2 Look again at the planning you did in Activity 3. Compare it with a grid written by another student in your class. Do you need to make any improvements to the points, evidence or explanations? Make notes to show any changes you would like to make.

_____

_____

_____

3 Write up the points as paragraphs in answer to the sample examination question in Activity 3, using your revised plan. Remember to refer back to the mark scheme to help you achieve the top mark.

_____

_____

_____

_____

_____

_____

_____

4 Now compare your full response with a different student from before. Ask them for some feedback on your response and then write some extra sentences, perhaps including additional examples and better use of the PEE technique, to improve your answer and to move it up to the next band.

_____

_____

Band	Description
3	• Some comparisons and links • Some evaluation of the different ways of expressing meaning and achieving effects • Selection of examples is valid but undeveloped
4	• Generally sound comparisons and links • Some clear evaluation of the different ways of expressing meaning and achieving effects • Selection of examples is mostly appropriate; shows some support of the points being made
5	• Sound comparisons and links • Some clear evaluation of the different ways of expressing meaning and achieving effects • Selection of examples is appropriate; shows some support of the points being made

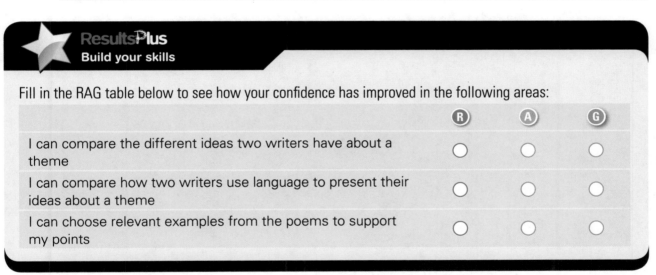

ResultsPlus
Build your skills

Fill in the RAG table below to see how your confidence has improved in the following areas:

	R	A	G
I can compare the different ideas two writers have about a theme	○	○	○
I can compare how two writers use language to present their ideas about a theme	○	○	○
I can choose relevant examples from the poems to support my points	○	○	○

Published by Pearson Education Limited, a company incorporated in England and Wales, having its registered office at Edinburgh Gate, Harlow, Essex, CM20 2JE. Registered company number: 872828

Edexcel is a registered trademark of Edexcel Limited

Text © Pearson Education Limited 2011

The rights of Janet Beauman, Alan Pearce, Racheal Smith and Pam Taylor to be identified as authors of this work have been asserted by them in accordance with the Copyright, Designs and Patent Act 1988.

First published 2011

15 14 13 12 11
10 9 8 7 6 5 4 3 2 1

British Library Cataloguing in Publication Data

A catalogue record for this book is available from the British Library.
ISBN 978 1 846909 44 3

Designed and typeset by Juice Creative Limited, Hertfordshire

Printed and bound in Spain by Grafos S. A.

Picture Credits
Cover image: iStockphoto: Krzysztof Kwiatkowski

Acknowledgements
We would like to thank Tony Farrell and Polly Hennessy for their invaluable help in the development of this title.

We are grateful to the following for permission to reproduce copyright material:

Extracts pages 8, 11, 17, 25, 32, 97, 98 and 105 from *To Kill a Mockingbird* by Harper Lee, published by William Heinemann. Reprinted by permission of The Random House Group Ltd; Extracts pages 8, 10, 16, 24, 32, 96, 98 and 104 from *Of Mice and Men*, Copyright © John Steinbeck, 1937, 1965. Reproduced by permission of Penguin Books Ltd. From OF MICE AND MEN by John Steinbeck, copyright 1937, renewed © 1965 by John Steinbeck. Used by permission of Viking Penguin, a division of Penguin Group (USA) Inc.; Extracts pages 72, 74, 80, 82 and 88 from *Animal Farm* by George Orwell (Copyright © George Orwell, 1945) by permission of Bill Hamilton as the Literary Executor of the Estate of the Late Sonia Brownell Orwell and Secker & Warburg Ltd. Excerpts from ANIMAL FARM by George Orwell, copyright 1964 by Harcourt, Inc. and renewed 1974 by Sonia Orwell, reprinted by permission of the publisher; Poetry page 111 and 120 from 'Orkney/This Life', *This Life, This Life: Selected Poems 1970–2006*, Bloodaxe Books (Greig, A 2006); Poetry page 111 from 'A Consumer's Report', Collected Poems, Oxford University Press (Porter, P. 1983); Poetry page 111 from 'City Jungle', *The Apple Raid*, Macmillan Children's Books (Corbett, P. 2001); Poetry page 112 from 'The Warm and the Cold' (Hughes, T), Faber & Faber, Copyright re estate of Ted Hughes; Poetry page 112 from 'I am the Wind', http://1-poem.com/i_am_the_ wind_personification_exercise.htm, 1-poem.com, Copyright Dr Silvia Hartmann, www.1-poem.com; Poetry page 113 from 'The City' (Hughes, L), *Collected Poems of Langston Hughes*, Alfred A Knopf/Vintage, David Higham Associates Ltd; Poetry page 114 from 'The Fog' by FR McCreary from *Opening Eyes: A Poetry Collection*, Cambridge University Press (Phillips, J); Poetry page 120 from 'Valentine' is taken from Mean Time by Carol Ann Duffy, published by Anvil Press Poetry in 1993; Poetry page 128 from 'One Flesh', *New Collected Poems*, Carcanet Press Ltd (Jennings, E 1987), David Higham Associates Ltd; Poetry page 128 from 'O What is that Sound', *Look, Stranger!* Faber & Faber (Auden, W. H. 2001), Copyright © 1936, 2001, The Estate of W. H. Auden; Poetry page 128 from 'Cape Town Morning', *Seasonal Fires: New and Selected Poems*, Copyright © 1997, 2006 by Ingrid de Kok. Reprinted with the permission of Seven Stories Press, www.sevenstories. com; Poetry page 128 from 'Zero Hour', *Earth Shattering: ecopoems*, Bloodaxe Books (Sweeney, M 2007); Poetry page 128 from 'One World Down the Drain', *Earth Shattering: ecopoems*, Bloodaxe Books (Rae, S 2007).

Every effort has been made to contact copyright holders of material reproduced in this book and we apologise for any unintentional omissions. Any omissions will be rectified in subsequent printings if notice is given to the publishers.